CARMEN
KEEP YOUR EYES Open!

Mark Oliver

2008

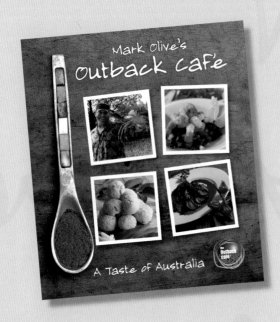

Publisher Paul Myers

Graphic Design Shannon O'Neill

Production Angela Noble

Project Managers Tanya Buchanan and Carla Daly

Photography John Brawley, with additional photos by Susan Evans, Jeremy Simons (cover backgrounds, page 6 et al), Don Fuchs (page 4) and Tourism NT

Text Bob Deere, Mike and Gayle Quarmby

Recipes Mark Olive. Assisted by Greg Reum and Yolanda Mauro

Administrator Roy Smith

Sales and Marketing Paul Deeming

Published By R.M. Williams Classic Publications ABN 81 223 753 104

A partnership between R.M.Williams Holdings Pty Ltd and Straight Arrow Communications Pty Ltd. Suite 13, 235 Spit Road, Mosman NSW 2088. Phone + 61 2 9969 8866 fax + 61 2 9969 8566.

In association with Mark Olive Pty Ltd, PO Box 6, Sandringham VIC 3191. Phone + 61 3 9585 8330 fax + 61 3 9585 8332.

Printed in China by APOL

ISBN 0-9775585-2-5

RRP $19.95

Proudly supported by

RMW CLASSIC PUBLICATIONS

www.theoutbackcafe.com

Tourism Australia

www.australia.com

Contents

Foreword

The Outback Café Cookbook will whet your appetite for Australia and the tastes of Australian food. The cookbook presents the outback communities, breathtaking Australian landscapes and spectacular cuisine.

Australia's premier indigenous chef, Mark Olive, offers the sights and tastes of the Australian bush. The variety, freshness and colour of Australian native foods are captured in his exciting collection of recipes. Evocative photographs of the dishes and locations from which the ingredients come provide every page with the magical atmosphere of Australia. These delicious, easy-to-follow recipes and glorious photographs bring unique Australian outback flavours into every kitchen.

This publication will serve as a valuable guide for people interested in Australia's spectacular landscapes and in the fabulous flavours of Australian bush foods. In addition, a wealth of information is presented on Australian tourism, indigenous communities and Australian native produce.

The Outback Café aims to provide many benefits to indigenous Australian communities by encouraging tourism and employment opportunities, as well as assisting the growth of the small business that the native food industry creates and supports.

The Outback Café cookbook will also provide enormous benefits to the Australian tourism industry. By showcasing Australia, from the breathtaking Great Ocean Road in Victoria to the world heritage Kakadu National Park, the cookbook promotes and explores many of the unique regions of Australia.

To all the people responsible for this publication, I offer my sincere congratulations. They have recognised the importance of such a book to Australian tourism, indigenous Australian communities and small business.

We support Mark Olive and The Outback Café, and thank him for supporting tourism in Australia, as well as assisting in the creation of opportunities for indigenous Australians.

The Hon Fran Bailey MP
Minister for Small Business and Tourism

Mark Olive

Mark Olive aka "The Black Olive" is Australia's first high profile indigenous chef. He has a passion about bringing the vibrant colours and earthy tastes of ancient outback flavours and food to the dining tables across the country, and around the world. His dream is to see the wonderful, natural produce of the outback used in everyday cooking.

Mark Olive's passion for food began at an early age when growing up with his family in Wollongong on the breathtaking scenic coastline of the Illawarra Region. Regularly, the family would return to their homeland Bundjalung, Cabbage Tree Island and Casino on the Northern Rivers of NSW, where he would watch his aunts and mother prepare food. "Occasionally they cooked with traditional foods like wattleseed and lemon myrtle and I was fascinated by the process." Mark says. "When I left school, it came down to being a mechanic or cooking, and after doing work experience in a kitchen, I chose cooking."

There in Wollongong, Mark trained under Italian chef Rino Collechia, an amazing chef who nurtured Mark's passion for food. After finishing his apprenticeship Mark was employed in diverse areas of cooking; in clubs, theatre restaurants and à la carte kitchens, as well as the occasional wedding and birthday party within the region.

In the late 1980s he began experimenting with bush foods, from where the first seeds were sown in his now rising career. After the death of his mother to kidney disease in 1992, Mark moved to Sydney and continued his diverse career in kitchens around Sydney. At the end of 1993 Mark was searching for a career change and spent time working in community television.

Mark's involvement with film and TV brought a new twist to his career – one that has enabled him to successfully combine his talents with food and communications. After undertaking an Indigenous film course at the Australian Film Television and Radio School (AFTRS) under Uncle Lester Bostock, in 1995 Mark landed a job with Baz Lurhmann as a runner for the initial pitches for 'Romeo and Juliet' minding Leonardo De Caprio and Natalie Portman (Leonardo got the role as Romeo, but Claire Danes was eventually chosen for the role of Juliet).

In 1996, Mark was chef at his Sydney restaurant 'The Midden' which featured indigenous ingredients. The restaurant remained open for about 18 months ("it was way ahead of its time", Mark reflects) but during its brief life Mark's profile began to rise.

The next year saw the start of an indigenous film series titled 'Shifting Sands'. Mark adapted and pitched a short story, 'Passing Through' which was chosen for the series and was later shown at festivals locally and overseas.

'It was then that I decided I loved the film and television industry', Mark says. "I moved to Melbourne in 1998 to attend an indigenous theatre course at Swinburne University learning the art of writing, presenting and set design, and started developing the concept for an indigenous cooking show."

In 2001 Mark was accepted into the Victorian College of the Arts (VCA) where he was awarded a Bachelor of Arts in Film and Television, and later appeared regularly on the ABC TV series 'Message Stick' as their resident chef.

In his television show on the Lifestyle Channel, Mark takes viewers on a breathtaking tour across Australia – visiting Aboriginal communities where local people help him to find bush foods and pass on their knowledge, gained over thousands of years, about how to use them.

He introduces some tantalising flavours – lemon and aniseed myrtle, wild lime, mountain pepper, native thyme, lemon aspen, acacia seeds, quandong, rivermint, saltbush, bush tomatoes, muntries (bush bananas), tanami apples and many more.

He uses his skills as a modern chef to cook with these ingredients, blending bush flavours with international cuisines to create his own mouth-watering recipes and, in doing so, a stunning new approach to food.

All Mark's recipes and ingredients are readily available. There's nothing that any home cook can't produce. Some of his recipes feature kangaroo, emu and crocodile – but Mark says native herbs and spices go just as well with beef, lamb, chicken, seafoods, pasta and produce procurable at any supermarket or specialty store.

It all adds up to a feast of flavours and a feast of scenery. Touch, taste and experience – all that Australia has to offer from the red plains of the deserts to the flavours of a unique style of cooking that blends the contemporary with the ancient.

The Outback Pride Project

The Outback Café range of native herbs and spices is sourced directly from indigenous community farms through the Outback Pride Project. The Outback Café range is available through the website *www.theoutbackcafe.com*

"...jobs and training for indigenous Australians."

The Outback Pride Project was created by Mike and Gayle Quarmby of Reedy Creek in South Australia. It was born from a need to take a positive journey following the tragic loss of a 20 year old son. They wanted to make a difference in the lives of other 20 year olds, and felt that the most at need were the indigenous youth on remote communities.

Gayle's family involvement with traditional communities goes back to 1932, when her father Rex Battarbee travelled in a model T Ford to the central Australian outback settlement of Hermannsburg south west of Alice Springs. He was a watercolour artist in search of the great outback landscape. Rex was moved by the plight of indigenous Australians, who at that time struggled with cultural change, and had very few prospects for employment and healthy lifestyle. While at Hermannsburg Rex met a young camel team worker called Albert. They developed a strong friendship, which resulted in Rex training Albert as a landscape artist. With Rex's mentorship, Albert Namatjira and kin, became known around the world as the Hermannsburg watercolour movement. From those beginnings, the current aboriginal art industry was created and has provided valuable careers for many remote indigenous artists.

Gayle grew up with the Eastern Arrente people of the Hermannsburg and Alice Springs area, and fondly remembers gathering bushfood with the women and children. This cultural connection has been a vital link in the Outback Pride project development.

Mike Quarmby has had a lifetime of experience in the commercial horticultural industry, and during that time, was particularly involved in the development of arid zone horticultural practices. Mike's talent for innovation in species development, plant propagation, cultivation and new product development has been an integral part of this project. Reedy Creek Nursery, in South Australia's South East, which is owned by Mike and Gayle has provided the commercial base for research and development of all facets of the project. Mike and Gayle felt that their combined skills could provide a platform for the development of a bushfood industry which should move towards their vision of: "Jobs and Training for Indigenous Australians". They saw that the bushfood industry should be in a parallel place alongside the aboriginal art industry. Both these industries should have a unique cultural and commercial ownership by indigenous Australians.

The journey over the past six years has taken Mike and Gayle on a complex and interesting pathway. The initial part was spent in the outback with aboriginal people researching the bushfood species and mapping the best types relative to their commercial potential. Invaluable support was given by their good friend and botanist Peter Latz. The next part was to create the systems of propagation and cultivation for up to 64 bushfood species. That process is ongoing and consumes a large amount of Mike's time. The systems developed were then put into practice on numerous trial sites spread over South Australia and Northern Territory. A big part of the Quarmbys' vision was to incorporate accredited training for

participants in the project. Groups of participants have been brought from communities to Reedy Creek Nursery to be able to access real industry work experience. A partnership between Reedy Creek Nursery and Regional TAFE South Australia supports this skill development process.

They decided initially to self fund the project and have given five years of their time at no cost to indigenous communities. After many years of mentoring, developing and supplying the plants, and helping the communities set up the growing systems, Mike and Gayle have been joined by various government departments, including ILC, DEWR, Works South Australia, Department of the Premier and Cabinet South Australia, Regional TAFE South Australia and Nganampa Health Council, who have also provided valuable support to the communities involved.

In order to guarantee an outcome for the participating indigenous communities, a co-op like value adding arm was developed. Combining the knowledge of traditional uses of the bushfoods with western food practices, the end use products are available under the brand name "Outback Pride". The supply chain for Outback Café is through the Outback Pride project. The group of Aboriginal communities forming the Outback Pride network represents the largest bushfood growing organisation in Australia.

Adelaide CDEP

Adelaide Community Development Employment Program

Adelaide Community Development Employment Program facility, situated in Kaurna country in the north of Adelaide's metropolitan area, is the distribution centre for the Outback Pride range of bushfood products and is the food service centre for South Australia and Northern Territory.

The marketing team, Allison and Renee Watkins, distribute product to retailers, restaurants and manufacturers as well as conducting promotional events and tasting demonstrations. Adelaide Community Development Employment Program also operates a farm block at Angle Vale that produces muntries and native limes for the bushfood market.

Amata

Anangu Pitjantjatjara Yankunytjatjara Lands

Amata community is situated in the magnificent Musgrave Ranges in far north-west South Australia, about 200 kilometres south east of Uluru, Northern Territory. Amata is a small Aboriginal community of some 500 people who hold strong links to traditional culture and language (Pitjantjatjara).

The people decided to join the Outback Pride project network and build a bushfoods garden in the centre of town. The purpose of the garden has been to provide a ready supply of fresh bushfoods for community consumption, with surpluses sold into the Outback Pride supply chain. Since the beginning of the project at Amata, the people have shown great pride in their work and the result is a beautifully maintained and successful enterprise.

The project construction at Amata has been supported by Community Development Employment Program and horticultural training for participants has been provided by Regional TAFE South Australia. The Department of Premier and Cabinet South Australia's special projects unit has funded the project which has been co-ordinated and managed by Mike and Gayle Quarmby.

Community health, training and positive activity have been the strengths of the project. The bushfoods grown at Amata are desert raisins (kampurarpa), passionberries (wiriny wirinypa), marsdenia (kalkula), desert yams, native orange (umpultjai), and rock fig (Illi).

Bookyana Bushfoods

Yorke Peninsula

The Bookyana Bushfoods enterprise is situated on Ron and Liz Newchurch's property at Port Victoria on the Yorke Peninsula in South Australia. This maritime environment is ideal for growing bushfood herbs used in the Outback Café recipes. Ron and family are of the Narungga group and have an extended family base who help with the horticultural project. Because of the exposure to the sea winds, the herbs are grown in shade house conditions. The quandong orchard, however, is protected by the shade house structure.

The Indigenous Land Council funded the infrastructure costs and Community Development Employment Program supplied labour costs. Regional TAFE South Australia has providing the training, along with several work experience/training visits to Reedy Creek. Mike and Gayle Quarmby have designed, set up and mentored the project and provided the link to the Outback Pride market supply chain.

The Newchurch family group has progressed with the bushfoods project with dedication, hard work and real future focus, and a positive new industry model has been developed for indigenous communities. Ron Newchurch has been appointed as board member to the national industry body of the Australian Native Food Industry as the representative for all the Australian indigenous bushfoods growers.

Currently, Bookyana Bushfoods Inc is planning towards major expansion of its bushfoods production site to cater for new market requirements.

Burrandies

Mount Gambier

The Burrandies bushfood garden is located in Mount Gambier in South Australia's lower south-east near the Victorian border. The traditional people from this area were of the Boandik/Bunganditj language group and the Burrandies organisation caters for employment and training for indigenous people from surrounding districts.

Mount Gambier is the site of dormant volcanoes, including the famous Blue Lake crater and because of this the area has rich volcanic soil. Coupled with a cool wet climate this makes the site ideal for the cultivation of Tasmanian mountain pepper, sea parsley and muntries.

The plants are thriving, and the community will progressively increase its production for the Outback Pride supply chain. Mike and Gayle Quarmby have assisted the Burrandies group with planning, establishment and horticultural mentoring of the project, and more recently have provided a hot house structure for propagation of Australian native trees and shrubs.

Training is provided by Regional TAFE South Australia, and the team from Burrandies have participated in work experience at Reedy Creek several times over the past three years.

Dinahline Community

Ceduna

The town of Ceduna is located on the far west coast of South Australia at the beginning of the Great Australian Bight. It is a focal fishing and whale spotting area famous for its whiting and oysters. The Dinahline community is located just to the west of Ceduna and the dry sandy soils are ideal for the production of arid zone bushfoods.

The Dinahline group has been growing bushfoods for many years with the support of Mike and Gayle Quarmby, Regional TAFE South Australia and other state government bodies.

Mike and Gayle Quarmby have always admired the diligence and hard work ethic of the bushfoods team at Dinahline, and they have been proud to have been associated with the community in their endeavours.

As part of the Wirangu language group, the Dinahline community has had a long- term and important connection to quandongs (bra) and are proud of their success with this species. The crops of desert raisins and marsdenia have also been successful, the produce of which has not only gone into the Outback Pride supply chain, but has also been part of the supply to the remote traditional communities.

Meningie CDEP

Meningie Community Development Employment Program "Old Church Block"

The township of Meningie is located at the edge of the world heritage Coorong National Park in the south-east of South Australia. The fresh water Lake Albert provides a picturesque backdrop to the community, with pelicans paddling in the still waters. This is Narrindjeri country and the Trevorrow family operates the Wilderness Lodge at Hacks Point and Camp Coorong, near Meningie that provides an indigenous tourism experience with pre-booked bushfood tours and basket-weaving workshops.

The Meningie Community Development Employment Program operates the bushfood garden at the "Old Church Block ". With State government funding for infrastructure and Regional TAFE providing training, Mike and Gayle Quarmby have provided the horticultural expertise and mentoring and links to the market through the Outback Pride supply chain.

Local indigenous plant species grown on this rich sandy loam site are muntries, sweet appleberries and sea parsley/celery. This garden has also been a useful training site for group members studying horticulture.

Mimili

Anangu Pitjantjatjara Yankunytjatjara Lands

Mimili Community is in the far north west of South Australia in the stunning Everard Ranges. Mimili was the first community in the Anangu Pitjantjatjara Yankunytjatjara Lands to build a bushfoods garden with the help of Mike and Gayle Quarmby. Right from the beginning it was obvious that the people at Mimili had great enthusiasm for the project, which has also provided the advantage of having fresh bushfoods close at hand for most of the year.

The bushfood plants at Mimili have thrived and have shown how well native plants can perform under cultivation. Each month Mike and Gayle spend time at Mimili and have developed a close relationship with the people. They are always pleased to pick up quality bushfoods harvested by the bushfood team.

The project construction at Mimili has been supported by Community Development Employment Program and horticultural training for participants has been assisted by Regional TAFE South Australia. The Department of Premier and Cabinet South Australia's special projects unit has funded the project, which has been co-ordinated and managed by Mike and Gayle Quarmby.

Bushfoods grown at Mimili are desert raisins (kampurarpa), quandongs (mangata), tanami apples (ngaru), marsdenia (kalkula), desert yams, native orange umpultjai), rock fig (illi) and desert limes.

Nepabunna Community

Flinders Ranges

Nepabunna Community is in the magnificent Gammon Ranges of the upper Flinders Ranges of central South Australia. The Adynyamathanha people of this area have strong links to their traditional bush foods and particularly favour quandongs (uti), native orange (Iga Warta) and marsdenia (myakka). This area is classified as true desert country, with an average rainfall of 200mm per annum, and the soil is not much more than bull dust.

The bushfoods plot was established in late 2003 with the full support of Mike and Gayle Quarmby and with infrastructure support from the South Australian government. The project faced many challenges, not the least was the 45 degrees plus heat at the time of set up, and very poor soil and water supply. Despite this, the project progressed well until March the following year when a locust plague stripped every piece of vegetation from the district, including the bushfoods garden. Full credit to Kelvin Johnson and the team, who didn't give up and the following season produced the best quality desert raisins and Tanami apples in the industry.

The Nepabunna community has a long-term link with stock work and continues its love of horses. The community offers horse trail riding through some of the most beautiful arid zone range country in South Australia.

The bushfood crops grown at Nepabunna are desert raisins, Tanami apples, passionberries, marsdenia, native orange, bush cucumbers and quandongs.

Pukatja

Ernabella - Anangu Pitjantjatjara Yankunytjatjara Lands

The community of Pukatja was the site of the Presbyterian mission at Ernabella, in Central Australia. It was founded in 1937 and was handed to community administration in the mid 1970s. This community is historically at the centre of the Anangu Pitjantjatjara Yankunytjatjara Lands, and had a focus in its early days on the development of the Aboriginal art and craft industry under the guidance of Winifred Hilliard.

Pukatja is situated in the most beautiful of settings in the rugged Musgrave Ranges on the edges of a usually dry riverbed. Pukatja has a true central Australian arid climate, with dry cool winters and a hot summer wet season.

During 2006, the people of Pukatja began building a bushfood production plot on a saltbush flood plain close to the town centre. The project, with the support and planning of Mike and Gayle Quarmby, has a focus on education with strong links to the local school and Regional TAFE South Australia. It is being funded by the Department of the Premier and Cabinet South Australia.

The bushfood crops being planted at Pukatja are desert raisin (kampurarpa), tanami apples (ngaru), passionberries (wirriney wirinypa), marsdenia (kalkula) and quandongs (mangata).

Reedy Creek Nursery

Kingston, South Australia

Reedy Creek nursery is a commercial propagating nursery owned and run by Mike and Gayle Quarmby 20 kilometres south of Kingston in the south-eastern Limestone Coast area of South Australia. The core business at the nursery is native plant production for revegetation and forestry as well as grape rootling and grafting production and growing seedlings for various industries.

The nursery was built to utilise the abundant underground water supply and because of its proximity to the "green triangle" horticultural areas of South Australia's rich south-east. The facilities include sophisticated propagation and production hot houses, and has seeding capacity for up to 140,000 seedlings a day.

When Mike and Gayle decided to create the philanthropic Outback Pride project, they realised that a way to generate outcomes for remote indigenous people was to use the commercial base at Reedy Creek to develop and fund this emerging industry. Reedy Creek nursery has the skilled staff and facilities to support the enormous amount of research and development required for the Outback Pride project.

Systems are developed at Reedy Creek for the propagation and cultivation of the bushfood plants which are planted in Aboriginal communities throughout South Australia and in the Northern Territory. This has resulted in a coordinated planting program for the supply chain and guarantees the best plant selections are used at all times. The produce from community gardens returns to Reedy Creek to be value added before being dispatched to indigenous distributors throughout Australia.

In order to provide a secure outcome for the bushfood gardens on each community, the brand name Outback Pride was created in December 2001. Over the past five years facilities have been built for post-harvest handling and manufacture of value added Outback Pride products. The range of bushfood products includes a large variety of sauces, relishes, dressings, meat pies and a comprehensive food service line. The dried native herb range is now available through the Outback Café website.

To facilitate the long-term industry growth for indigenous communities, Mike and Gayle Quarmby have always made available the Reedy Creek facilities for work experience and specialised horticultural training in bushfood cultivation.

Tangglun Piltengi Yunti

Pomberuk - Murray Bridge

Tangglun Piltengi Yunti farm is situated at Murray Bridge on the lower reaches of the Murray River in South Australia and the Murray Bridge area is a prominent producer of market garden vegetables for the Adelaide and interstate markets. The TPY farm site has a diverse potential, with glasshouses and production areas set aside for the bushfoods project.

TPY began growing bushfoods with the help of Mike and Gayle Quarmby in 2001. The garden includes muntries, desert raisins and wattleseed production, as well as a supply of tomatoes and chillies into the Outback Pride manufacturing network.

This is Narrindjeri country, and the community is also fortunate to have the "Old Pump House" on the river bank in the township of Murray Bridge. The facility is called Pomberuk which includes a bush tucker café overlooking the river, a gift shop and an art gallery with an indigenous interpretive centre.

Wilcannia

Western New South Wales

Wilcannia is a regional township in far western New South Wales, close to the Darling River and 190 kilometres from Broken Hill.

The Murdi Paaki Regional Enterprise Corporation is establishing a bushfood production site on the fertile alluvial flood plain of the Darling River. This location is ideal for the commercial production of bushfoods and will provide a training and enterprise opportunity for the local indigenous group.

The bushfoods being planted include wattleseed – acacia retinodes (wirilda), desert limes, native oranges, desert raisins, passionberries, Tanami apples and marsdenia. This site will give a climatic crop timing variation from the other arid zone production areas and therefore be a valuable link in the annual Outback Pride supply chain program.

Cooking with Indigenous Herbs, Spices & Bush Fruits

saltbush

Atriplex nummularia from the Chenopodiaceae family

Old Man Saltbush is a familiar sight over large areas of the dry inland of Australia. It is a sprawling grey/blue shrub up to three metres in height, sometimes spreading to five metres wide. It is a long-living plant, growing strongly after periods of summer rain where it grows long tassles of flowering seed heads. In old times, indigenous Australians mostly collected the minute saltbush seeds to grind and roast for damper.

A special selection of Old Man Saltbush has been developed by Outback Pride's Mike Quarmby for the gourmet food industry. Mike was involved in providing millions of saltbush seedlings to the revegetation and pastoral industry to rehabilitate degraded land. He soon realised that overgrazing had removed the best types of saltbush from rangelands and only the bitter leafed plants were left. Mike undertook a lengthy journey to find natural stands of saltbush that had been protected from overgrazing. He established selection trial plots, with the end result being a much improved saltbush that is quite different in flavour to the hard-grown wild plant. When grown in hot house conditions, it provides a large-leafed vegetable with a natural range of mineral salts, antioxidants, calcium and 27 percent crude protein.

The large fresh blanched saltbush leaves can be used as a wrap around meat or fish, in salads or as a leafy bed to grilled meat or vegetables. The dried saltbush flakes are a wonderful addition to bread, grills, pasta and as a pot herb. The herb mix Desert Flakes contains saltbush with other unique Australian spices to give a medley of wonderful outback flavours.

To order dried saltbush, simply go to *www.theoutbackcafe.com*

Seared Kangaroo Fillet with Illawarra Plum Sauce

Ingredients

- 250g kangaroo fillet or beef
- 100g Illawarra plums or blueberries
- 2 dstspns honey
- 1 cup red wine
- 1 dstspn butter
- 1 dstspn flour
- 1 cup water
- Native pepper and saltbush
  or salt and pepper
- 2 handfuls of warrigal greens or rocket

Method

Pre-heat oven to 200°C. To prepare the sauce, melt butter in a saucepan and stir in the flour. Cook for 3-4 minutes over a medium heat until lightly coloured. Whisk in the wine and water to achieve a smooth texture. Add the pepper, Illawarra plums and honey, simmer for 5 minutes.

Coat a frypan with olive oil and sear the fillet until golden brown on the outside. Place in oven for a further 5 minutes.

While the fillet is cooking, blanch the warrigal greens in boiling water for 40 seconds, remove and squeeze out excess water.

To serve, place the warrigal greens on the plate, top with sliced fillet and coat with the plum sauce.

Bush Cucumber

Cucumis melo – agrestis species, Cucurbitaceae Family

This annual vine occurs in isolated areas of western Queensland and south-east Northern Territory. Although it would have once been common through most of the central arid zone, like passionberries, bush cucumbers have been the victim of introduced grazing animals which find the aroma and taste of the cucumbers irresistible. Unlike emus, which love this fruit, introduced stock and feral animals fully digest the seed and therefore take it permanently from the area.

Like its cousins in the melon family, bush cucumbers enthusiastically climb up and along rocks, logs and low shrubs, sometimes spreading up to three metres with long trailing runners. The pale green leaves are roughly triangular, about 50mm across and feel a bit like sandpaper. The tiny yellow flowers are born at each leaf node and prolifically form fruit that resemble green spotted pigeons' eggs.

This was a favourite fruit of indigenous people of the desert as it not only tastes great, but the fruit will keep in a cool dry environment for many months. Bush cucumbers are currently being cultivated at Nepabunna Community in the Flinders Ranges of South Australia.

Bush cucumbers can be used in salads and dressings, or pickled for use in relishes.

Bush Pasta Salad

Ingredients

- 50g rehydrated desert raisins
- ½ a red onion, thinly sliced
- 1 cup roasted macadamia nuts
- 2 large handfuls of rocket
- 2 roma tomatoes, chopped
- 1 bush or Lebanese cucumber
- 2 cups cooked penne pasta

Dressing

- 4 dstspns macadamia nut oil or olive oil
- 3 dstspns each of balsamic vinegar
- Juice of 1 lemon
- Desert flakes

Method

Finely chop desert raisins. Deseed and chop the bush cucumber.

In a large bowl, place rocket, tomatoes, cucumber, onion, nuts, desert raisins and pasta; toss to combine.

To make the dressing, mix oil, balsamic vinegar, lemon juice and desert flakes in a small bowl.

Pour over salad, tossing gently to combine.

Serves 2.

Desert Limes

Eremocitrus glauca – Rutaceae Family

This small slender and spiny tree grows naturally over the inland dry areas of south-western Queensland and western NSW, with a small pocket of habitat in the Southern Flinders Ranges in South Australia. It is a true citrus with slender upward facing leaves 5–8 millimetres across and producing white flowers in spring. The fruit are like tiny lemons with a porous rind and juicy but sour centre. The trees often appear in groups formed by suckering, particularly where heavy grazing has occurred.

Desert limes are normally slow growing, like most Australian native citrus species, but when grown in cultivation they are usually grafted, which makes them faster maturing, more productive and less likely to sucker.

Desert limes were eaten raw by indigenous people, but most Europeans found them too sour and tended to use them for summer drinks or marmalade jam. Increasingly, gourmet chefs have discovered their unique wild lime flavour to be a welcome addition to fish sauces, salad dressings, flavoured butter and a multitude of desserts, not the least desert lime sorbet.

Smoked Eel Patties

Ingredients

- 1 smoked eel
- 1 cooked sweet potato
- 1 tsp lemon myrtle
- 2 dstspns chopped desert lime
- 1 egg separated
- 1 tsp mountain pepper
- 1 handful chopped dill
- 2 tsps cornflour

Method

Skin and debone the eel and break the meat up into a bowl. Add the cooked sweet potato and mash together. Add lemon myrtle, desert lime, egg yolk, mountain pepper, dill and cornflour, mix thoroughly. Roll the mix into small balls and flatten out to form patties then dust with a little cornflour. Heat a frying pan with a little oil and fry off patties until golden brown, remove from pan and drain on greaseproof paper.

Serves 6.

Kutjera - Desert Raisins

Solanum centrale - Solanacea Family

Kutjera (Kampurarpa – Pitjantjatjara language) is a small desert plant about 30 centimetres in height with grey to bronze leaves and attractive mauve/blue flowers that grows naturally throughout the central deserts from Tennant Creek, Northern Territory to Marla, South Australia.

It is part of the tomato family, which includes potatoes and capsicums. There are more than 100 species of solanums (wild tomatoes) in Australia, but only six are known to be edible. Kutjera – desert raisins, are the most well known and certainly the most consumed species of the so-called "bush tomatoes".

In the red sandy desert the plants grow quickly after summer rains, mainly from dormant rootstock that can last for many years between favourable seasons. The plant also responds and grows rapidly after soil disturbance (along roadsides) or after bushfires.

This arid land fruit has been a staple food of indigenous desert dwellers of Central Australia for thousands of years, and are a rich source of minerals, especially potassium. They are also high in Vitamin C.

The traditional way of harvesting is to collect the sun-dried fruits of the small bush in autumn/winter. In dried form, desert raisins can be stored for several years.

Desert Raisins are now being cultivated in commercial plots in indigenous communities in desert regions of Australia. With the use of waterwise irrigation systems, the fruiting cycle has been expanded to eight months instead of just two (as in the wild).

Outback Pride communities currently growing this fruit are Dinahline at Ceduna, South Australia, Nepabunna, in the Flinders Ranges of South Australia, and Mimili, Amata and Pukatja in the Anangu Pitjantjatjara Yankunytjatjara Lands of northern South Australia.

Kutjera – desert raisins – have a distinctive raisin/caramel introduction with a strong spicy after taste, making the fruit ideal for use when chopped into curries, salsas and as a crust on meat. Ground kutjera is an easy form of this spice for sprinkling on baked vegetables, and when used in sauces and bread mixes.

To order kutjera powder (desert raisins), simply go to *www.theoutbackcafe.com*

Kutjera Pasta

Ingredients

- 3 eggs, lightly beaten
- 300g plain flour
- 30ml olive oil
- Salt to taste
- 1 dstspn Kutjera Powder

Method

Place flour and salt in a bowl or onto a bench, make a well in the centre and add the eggs and oil. Mix to form a dough, then knead lightly adding more flour if the dough is sticky or soft. Wrap in cling wrap and rest for 1 hour.

Divide dough into 6 pieces and dust with flour, using a pasta machine or a rolling pin, roll each piece of dough out and allow to rest. Continue until the pasta sheets are 2 millimetres in thickness. Place pasta sheets onto a floured surface or cloth until required. Cut into desired shapes, cook and serve with a sauce of your choice.

Makes about 1kg of pasta.

Sea Parsley/Celery

Apium prostratum – Filiforme – Apiaceae Family

Sea Parsley or Sea Celery, as it is sometimes called, occurs all along the southern coastline of Australia. Its leaf form and plant dimensions vary quite considerably from place to place, but most commonly it has an appearance of shiny dark green parsley, and is in fact closely related to European parsley.

The significant difference is that it grows right on the coastline, often submerged by the incoming storm tides. It is the connection to the seafront, where it grows in composted sea weed and sand, that gives it its special flavour. Sea Parsley/Celery grows in a prostrate manner over rocky ledges and sandy ridges and its small white flower clusters give rise to large amounts of seed in the summer months. Although an annual, it has a resilient tap root like a carrot which gives it a semi-perennial capacity. It was identified by early Europeans as far back as Captain Cook – 1788, and provided a welcome flavour boost to soup and stews at the time.

This herb is currently being cultivated at Bookyana Bushfoods – Port Victoria, Meningie Community Development Employment Program, Burrandies Aboriginal Corp – Mt Gambier and Reedy Creek SE South Australia.

It can be used in soups, dressings, flavoured butter, with seafood and white sauces.

To order dried sea parsley, simply go to *www.theoutbackcafe.com*

Damper For Vegans with Eucalyptus Butter

Ingredients

- 500g self-raising wholemeal flour
- 15g sea parsley/sea celery
- 15-20ml macadamia nut oil
- 200ml approximately of soy milk
- 100g flaxseed or canola oil butter at room temperature
- 5 drops eucalyptus oil specific for cooking

Method

Pre-heat oven to 180°C. Combine flour and sea celery in a bowl. Add the oil and milk and mix together roughly using your hands, making sure not to overwork the mixture. Roll into a rough log and divide into handful sized balls. Place the damper balls onto a flour dusted baking tray and bake in oven for 15-20 minutes or until golden brown.

Serve with Eucalyptus Butter. To make butter, mix eucalyptus oil and butter in a small bowl.

Makes 12 dinner roll size dampers.

Lemon Myrtle Leaf

Backhousia citriodora – Myrtaceae Family

A beautiful Australian shrub naturally occurring in wetter coastal areas of northern NSW and southern Queensland, lemon myrtle grows up to three metres high and has graceful hanging branches of soft green leaves. The clusters of cream feathery flowers occur in autumn, creating a spectacular fragrant display. The plant is a great complement to any home garden in the wetter areas of Australia and it thrives in a rich well-drained position.

Most cultivation of this herb occurs near Lismore in NSW, although it is rapidly expanding into all temperate growing areas. Used fresh, the lemon myrtle leaf is a most versatile and refreshing herb.

For storage, the leaves are cool dried to prevent loss of essential oils and then ground and stored in a cool, dry place for later use.

Lemon myrtle is, without doubt, the most popular of Australia's native herbs, with its fresh fragrance of creamy lemon and lime. It complements so many culinary delights, from fish and chicken to ice cream and sorbet.

To order lemon myrtle leaf, simply go to *www.theoutbackcafe.com*

Lemon Myrtle Seafood with Crepes

Ingredients

- 12 fresh mussels
- 8 de-veined prawns
- 1 calamari tube
- 1 fillet of perch
- ½ cup white wine
- ½ cup cream
- Lemon juice
- ½ tsp lemon myrtle
- 5 finely chopped lemon aspens
- ½ tsp chopped parsley
- Salt and pepper to taste

Method

Clean mussels and remove beards. Cut perch into large cubes ensuring there are no bones. Cut calamari tube down the side and open, remove spine and clean thoroughly. Lightly score the inside of the flesh with a sharp knife in a diagonal pattern making sure not to cut through the outer skin. Once scored, cut the tube into long inch wide pieces. Heat a little oil into a pan. Once oil is hot, place calamari pieces skin side down into the hot pan and toss (the calamari should curl up into tubes). Add wine and cream and simmer for a few minutes. Add lemon juice, lemon myrtle, lemon aspens, chopped parsley, perch, mussels and salt and pepper to taste. Simmer for a further 5 minutes reducing the sauce. To make the crepes, place flour, milk, egg, salt and pepper into a large bowl and mix until smooth. Stir in the rice and spinach. Coat a frypan with oil. Pour enough crepe mix to coat the bottom of the pan, cook until just set, turn and cook the other side for 15 seconds or until golden. Repeat until batter is used. Spoon cooked seafood on one half of each crepe, fold the crepe over the seafood like an envelope and pour sauce over the top. Serve with salad and chips.
Serves 2.

Marsdenia

Marsdenia australis – Asclepiadaceae Family

This extraordinary vine grows on Acacias in most parts of arid Australia from Kalgoorlie to the far east coast. In fact, the name Kalgoorlie was derived from the local indigenous name for this plant – Kurgula. Around Alice Springs it is called Langkwe and in the Flinders Ranges it is Myakka.

Marsdenia has a long twining stem which often seems to appear from nowhere on its host tree, and for the untrained eye the marsdenia fruit often seems to be part of the tree or bush on which it is climbing. The leaves vary from thin and spiky in the Flinders Ranges to long and wide for most plants that grow around Alice Springs, and even broader northwards to the Gulf Country.

Marsdenia or "bush banana" as they have been called are really the "pantry of the desert", as they have four different edible parts.

The fruit is shaped like a small smooth avocado and has a wonderful flavour not unlike crunchy snow peas and zucchini when small, that becomes woody and fibrous when fully grown. The plant exudes a sweet white sticky sap when fruit or leaves are plucked from the stem, and the fruit contains high levels of thiamine.

The flowers are quite spectacular, with creamy succulent clusters of small cups, which are full of nectar when in full bloom. The flowers alone are a culinary treat, and can be eaten straight from the vine or as a garnish.

The fresh young leaves are great in salads and there is a yam or tuber in the ground at the base of the vine. The tuber carries the plant through droughts, just waiting for the next big rains. The vine also immediately responds after a bushfire.

Marsdenia are being grown on indigenous groups in cultivation at Nepabunna, Dinahline, Mimili, and Amata on trellises not unlike grape vines.

The marsdenia fruit are a wonderful green vegetable, boiled or microwaved with butter, lemon juice and mountain pepper, or sliced raw into salads, stir-fried or used whole into casseroles. Marsdenia flowers are special as a garnish for salads or make a spectacular addition to fruit salad.

Sweet Potato and Marsdenia Bake

Ingredients

- 2 tbsps butter
- 2 cloves garlic, crushed
- 2 leeks, trimmed, halved and sliced
- 1kg sweet potato, thinly sliced
- 600g marsdenias, halved
- 2 cups cream
- ½ cup chicken stock
- 1 tsp each of dried marjoram, oregano and ground pepperberry
- 1 tbsp each of dried basil and paprika
- 2 tbsps of grated parmesan

Method

Pre-heat oven to 180°C and lightly grease a large oval baking dish.

Heat butter in a frypan, add garlic and leek and sauté for 3-4 minutes until soft.

Layer half the sweet potato in the dish, top with the leeks, then the bush banana and finally layer with the remaining sweet potato.

Combine cream, chicken stock and herbs in a large jug and mix well. Pour over the potatoes and sprinkle with the parmesan cheese.

Bake for 1-1½ hours or until potatoes are tender (cover with foil if the top starts to brown too quickly).

Mountain Pepper Leaf & Native Pepperberry

Tasmania lanceolata - Winteraceae Family

The native pepperberry plant is naturally found in the cold high country in Southern NSW, Victoria and Tasmania. This attractive five-metre high tree has shiny dark green pointed leaves with scarlet stemlets. It has small cream waxy flowers that develop into dark charcoal brown pepper berries that are borne only by female plants. Because only half the plants bear fruit, and it takes several years to begin fruiting, the pepper berries are a high-value commodity.

It is fortunate that the leaves of the mountain pepper plant also have a distinctive flavour and are a more immediate commercial crop. It also makes an attractive and useful garden plant in cooler parts of southern Australia. Mountain pepper plants feature heavily in indigenous traditional uses in both cooking and for medicinal purposes.

Mountain pepper leaf and its berries are now being cultivated in plantations across the cooler parts of Australia. Burrandies Aboriginal Corporation at Mount Gambier, South Australia is producing mountain pepper for the Outback Pride growers' network.

Although native pepperberry can be used in the same way as conventional pepper, it has an added herbal dimension, especially towards the end of the palette. The dark pepper berries also infuse a rich plum colour to sauces.

The mountain pepper leaf has a more subtle, organic herbal flavour than the berry and is ideal when the intensity of the pepperberry is too dominant.

To order dried mountain pepper, simply go to *www.theoutbackcafe.com*

Mountain Pepper Fish & Chips

Ingredients

- 2 perch fillets
- Lemon myrtle, ground, for dusting
- Plain flour, for dusting
- 300ml macadamia or olive oil
- 1 sweet potato

Batter

- 1 cup self-raising flour
- 1 egg
- 2 dstspns vinegar
- 1 cup water or beer
- Saltbush
- Native mountain pepper

Method

To make the batter, whisk egg, vinegar, flour, water or beer and chopped saltbush in a medium bowl until smooth. Set aside.

Cut the sweet potato into chip portions, dry well with tea towel or paper towel. Fry chips in batches until brown and cooked through.

Meanwhile, mix the ground lemon myrtle and flour. Coat the fillets with the flour and then dip in the batter. Cook in hot oil until golden brown.

Serves 2.

Muntries

Kunzea pomifera - Myrtaceae family

The Muntries or Muntharis are a ground-hugging native plant of south-east South Australia, with radial branches spreading over sandy ground, sometimes up to three metres in all directions. It has small round leaves about 3-4 millimetres in diameter and profuse cream feathery flowers in spring. The fruit form in clusters and ripen in February and March.

Muntries hold a significant place in the historical diet of the Narrindjeri people of the Coorong in south-east South Australia. These fruit played a major part in the diet, not only when fresh, but also after being dried and stored for winter. They were often traded with other tribes, usually after being pounded into a paste, which was then dried — the original fruit bar!

The fruit, which tastes like apple with a juniper essence, are now cultivated extensively on low trellises and there are many clones selected for heavy fruit production, colour and flavour. Outback Pride communities growing muntries are Meningie Community Development Employment Program, Adelaide Community Development Employment Program, Burrandies Aboriginal Corporation at Mt Gambier and Tangglun Piltengi Yunti at Murray Bridge, South Australia.

The harvested fruit are sold fresh, frozen or dried and make a wonderful addition to sweet savoury dishes, jams, chutney or simply as a dessert with ice-cream.

?

Muntrie Berry Shake

Ingredients

- 4 cups milk
- 1 cup muntrie berries or other seasonal berries
- 2 dstspns plain yoghurt
- 2 dstspns honey
- Large scoop ice-cream

Method

Place all the ingredients into a blender. Blend for approximately 40 seconds or until smooth. Pour into chilled tall glasses.

Serves 2.

Native Basil

Plectranthus graveolens - Lamiaceae Famil

This attractive aromatic plant naturally occurs on rocky ledges and ridges in Queensland and the Northern Territory. With its velvety crinkled leaves and stunning spikes of violet flowers it is a welcome sight for bushwalkers in national parks, where even to brush up against the leaves releases a pleasant basil and sage aroma.

Native basil is a hardy and useful decorative plant now found in gardens throughout coastal regions of Australia.

Indigenous Australians used this plant for medicinal and ceremonial purposes, and early European settlers often called it the "Five Spice Plant" because of its delightful fragrant mix of basil, mint and sage.

Despite its distinctive aroma, it is not an overpowering herb and can be used liberally in dishes where sweet basil would be used. It especially complements any tomato, garlic or Mediterranean-based cuisine.

To order dried native basil, simply go to *www.theoutbackcafe.com*

Wallaby Lasagne

Ingredients

- Pre made lasagne sheets
  (or instant lasagne sheets)
- 1kg wallaby or beef mince
- 2 onions, chopped
- Tinned crushed tomatoes
- Native basil
- Saltbush
- Macadamia or olive oil

Basic béchamel sauce

- 4 tbsps plain flour
- 1 tbsp butter
- 2 cups milk
- Cheese, grated

Method

Pre-heat oven to 180°C. Heat oil in a frypan, cook onions until golden, add wallaby and fry until lightly browned. Add tomatoes and herbs and simmer for 20 minutes. Remove from heat and set aside to cool.

To make the white sauce, melt butter in a medium size saucepan, add sifted flour and mix well with a whisk to avoid lumps. Slowly add milk, stirring constantly until sauce boils. Remove from heat, leave for a few minutes to allow sauce to thicken. Line a baking dish with a layer of pasta, top with one-third of the wallaby mixture. Spread with one-third of the white sauce and sprinkle with grated cheese. Repeat layering, finishing with white sauce topped with grated cheese. Bake for 30-40 minutes or until cheese is golden brown.

Serves 6.

Native Thyme

Prostranthera rotundafolia – Lamiateae Family

This strongly aromatic bush is a native to south-east NSW, eastern Victoria and Tasmania. The plant was used by indigenous Australians for its medicinal properties. The bush grows to two metres high, with a showy display of lilac flowers on the tips in spring. It has very small round leaves in pairs attached to a multitude of stemlets. This plant is related to the Westringi and naturally occurs in cool moist gullies, particularly along riverbanks. It is now a very popular garden plant and can even be used as a low hedge.

Native thyme is a strong growing plant when well watered in a sheltered, well-drained position in acid to neutral soil conditions. As a pot plant, it provides a continuous supply of ready herb, and is easy to maintain with regular pruning. Commercially, native thyme is grown in shade house conditions with well-drained raised beds.

A small amount of native thyme makes a big difference to chicken, turkey, pork and lamb dishes.

To order native thyme, simply go to *www.theoutbackcafe.com*

Stuffed Eggplant

Ingredients

- 2 eggplants
- 1 cup chick peas, drained and rinsed
- 200g split peas
- 5 dstspns almond meal
- ½ cup bush tomatoes
- Juice of a lemon
- 5 dstspns roasted ground bunya nuts
- 1 dstspn fresh basil
- 1 dstspn native thyme
- 1 red onion, finely diced
- 2 celery sticks, diced
- 2 carrots, diced
- 1 red and 1 yellow capsicum, diced
- Rind of a lemon, finely chopped
- ¼ cup muntrie berries
- ½ cup water
- Macadamia nut oil

Method

Pre-heat oven to 180°C.

Cut the eggplants in half lengthwise. Scrape out the flesh with a spoon, leaving about ¼ inch flesh next to the skin. Finely chop the flesh and set aside for the filling. Place chickpeas, split peas, almond meal, bush tomatoes, lemon juice, ground bunya nuts, eggplant flesh, basil and native thyme into a blender. Blend to a smooth paste, adding a little water if necessary.

Place hollowed eggplant shells in the oven to soften for 5 minutes. Meanwhile, heat a little oil in a frypan and cook onions, celery, carrots, capsicum and lemon rind until golden. In a large bowl, mix cooked vegetables, eggplant paste and muntrie berries.

Spoon mixture into the eggplant shells and bake in oven for 20 minutes or until golden.

Serves 4.

Passionberry

Solanum cleistogamum – Solanaceae Family

A native of the central desert regions and another of Australia's many and varied wild tomatoes, passionberries are a real sweet surprise. This prickly groundcover has mid-green soft leaves about 2 centimetres wide and 5 centimetres long and are generally incurved. Small insignificant white to lilac flowers are often hidden in its tangled mass of creeping branches.

The amazingly sweet and aromatic fruit are generally 1 to 1.5 centimetres in diameter and hang in great numbers right at soil level under the plant. The fruit are ripe when creamy yellow and taste somewhere between banana, caramel and vanilla. When the fruit fully ripen and dry, they fall off the plant, where they are a delicacy for every small animal, bird or reptile that is attracted to the lure of the sweet fruit.

Passionberries have become rare in most of Central Australia because of widespread digestion by feral and station animals such as goats, donkeys, horses, cattle and camels which can smell the ripe fruit from kilometres away. These introduced grazers with double stomachs fully digest the seed, whereas prior to the introduction of these animals, emus did not fully digest the seed, but passed the scarified seed out with its own all-organic fertiliser.

Over the past few years Mike and Gayle Quarmby have introduced the species into cultivation. Several indigenous communities including those at Nepabunna, Amata and Reedy Creek are now producing the tasty fruit.

Dessert passion syrup made from passionberries is Australia's alternative to maple syrup, and is superb on pancakes, ice-cream or in milkshakes.

Indigenous Berry Shake

Ingredients

- ⅓ cup quandongs
- ⅓ cup muntrie berries
- ⅓ cup passionberries
- 1 dstspn bran
- 2 dstspns honey
- 2 dstspns yoghurt
- 1 scoop of ice-cream
- 1 litre milk (can substitute soy milk)

Method

Place all the ingredients into a blender. Blend for approximately 40 seconds or until smooth.

Pour into chilled glasses.

Serves 6.

Quandong

Santalum acuminatum – Santalaceae Family

A small desert tree up to four metres high with rough dark bark and pale green elongated hanging leaves, quandong trees use the root system of other trees, shrubs and grasses to supplement their own supply of nutrients and water, and as such will usually be found growing from the base of another tree. The cream flowers are small and cup shaped in clusters at the ends of the outer branchlets. The flowers form in late summer and, depending on the season, form fruit that is ready for harvest in early spring.

The bright scarlet shiny fruit is about 2 centimetres in diameter and contains one large nut or kernel that sometimes is only marginally smaller than the fruit.

Quandongs have been an important traditional Aboriginal fruit. Although somewhat tart, it is highly nutritious and contains twice the vitamin C of an orange. The kernel is also very nutritious, but indigenous Australians tended to mainly use this for medicinal purposes. The wood from the slow-growing trees was prized for making traditional bowls – pitti or coolamons. Quandong fruit feature heavily in Aboriginal mythology across all the desert regions of Australia.

Aboriginal communities growing quandongs in plantations are Mimili and Amata in the Anangu Pitjantjatjara Yankunytjatjara Lands of northern South Australia, Dinahline at Ceduna, Nepabunna in the Flinders Ranges and Bookyana at Port Victoria.

There is nothing yummier than quandong pie with cream ice-cream, quandong sauce glazed over roast lamb or pork, scones with quandong jam and cream, quandong and chilli dipping sauce with spring rolls or chicken wings... and the list goes on.

Wattleseed Creamed Meringue with Quandong Sauce

Ingredients

- 300ml thickened cream
- 3 tsps ground roasted wattleseed
- 6 small meringue cases
- 250g fresh quandongs or raspberries
- 3 dstspns caster sugar
- 3 dstspns raspberry jam

Method

Steep wattleseed in boiling water (to swell) and set aside to cool.

Whip cream until it peaks, stir through wattleseed and set aside in fridge.

Place quandongs or raspberries in saucepan with 2 cups of water. Stew until reduced by half. Add caster sugar and simmer for 5 minutes.

Add jam and simmer for a further 3-4 minutes. (TIP: You can use a hand-held food processor on this mixture for a smooth textured sauce).

To serve, top each meringue case with the wattleseed cream and drizzle with the quandong sauce.

Serves 6.

Rivermint

Mentha australis – Lamiateae Family

This rambling mint bush is found across south-eastern Australia in moist forests and around waterways. The thin, soft serrated pointed leaves grow in pairs on long running branches tipped with delicate mauve florets. This is a subtle Australian native herb with a taste and aroma of spearmint. Indigenous Australians also used this herb for medicinal purposes.

Rivermint is a summer-growing plant that thrives along riverbanks after flood, particularly in the Murray-Darling Basin waterways. It was enthusiastically embraced by early settlers and used with their roast lamb.

Commercial production of rivermint is being undertaken in shade house conditions with automatic irrigation systems and sequenced flush harvesting at Outback Pride's headquarters at Reedy Creek, South Australia.

Rivermint is ideal for use in meat sauces, salads, fruit drinks, infused tea and desserts.

To order dried rivermint, simply go to *www.theoutbackcafe.com*

Crusted Emu and Kangaroo Fillets

Ingredients

- 250g emu rump fillet
- 250g kangaroo fillet
  or 500g scotch fillet

Bush rub mixture

- ⅓ cup kutjera powder
- ⅓ cup mountain pepper
- ⅓ cup dried rivermint
- ⅓ cup wattleseed
- ⅓ cup native thyme
- ⅓ cup sea parsley

Sauce

- 1 cup muntries
- 1 onion, diced
- 2 dstspns butter
- 3 dstspns plain flour
- 2 cups beef stock
- ½ tsp mountain pepper
- ¼ cup of red wine
- Olive oil

Method

Pre-heat oven to 180˚C. Mix kutjera powder, mountain pepper, rivermint, wattleseed, native thyme and sea parsley in a bowl to make herb mix. Spread dry mix onto a plate. Rub emu and kangaroo fillets in a little olive oil and roll in the herb mix. Once completely covered in herbs lay fillets on an oiled baking tray and place in oven for 10-15 minutes or until cooked medium rare.

Meanwhile to make the sauce, melt butter in a saucepan until a nutty brown colour, add flour stirring vigorously. Slowly add stock stirring continuously, add wine and mountain pepper ensuring all lumps are dissolved.

Add muntries and stir through. Remove from heat.

Remove fillets from the oven and rest for a few minutes before slicing into medallions.

Place alternate medallions of emu and kangaroo on a plate and drizzle with sauce. Serve with roasted sweet potato mash and salad.

Serves 2.

Tanami Apples

Solanum chippendaleai - Solanaceae Family

A native to the central and western deserts of Australia, this robust and spectacular member of the bush tomato family can reach 1.5 metres in height and 2.5 metres in diameter, with bright silver grey leaves 3-5 centimetres wide and 8-10 centimetres long. The flowers are a dazzling show of bright purple and blue with hundreds of flowers on each bush at a time. The large golf ball-sized fruit hang from the bush on spiny stems, sometimes up to 15 centimetres long. The fruit ripen in autumn, turn a pale cream colour and will easily be twisted from their calyx. When the ripe fruit are cut in half they reveal a large number of black bitter seeds which take up all but a 4-5 millimetres outer layer of pale green flesh.

Tanami apples taste somewhat like a melon or zucchini and are a favourite of the indigenous people of Central Australia. Indigenous desert dwellers cut the fruit and remove the bitter seeds with a flat stick and place the half fruits inside each other and thread them onto a stick to dry. In this way the fruit can be stored or carried for long distances as a convenient travelling food.

Tanami apples are now being cultivated by indigenous groups at Nepabunna in the Flinders Ranges and at Mimili, Amata and Pukatja in the Anangu Pitjantjatjara Yankunytjatjara Lands of northern South Australia.

When dried and coarse ground tanami apples make a great addition to dukka, and are particularly tasty when fresh and stuffed with small spicy meat balls and placed on a skewer, then grilled on an open fire. Another favourite is when they are filled with chopped bacon and cheese and put under a griller to brown.

Tanami Apple Tartlet

Ingredients

- 8 Tanami apples or
  4 large Granny Smith apples
- 115g blanched almonds
- 2 tbsps plain flour
- 100g unsalted butter
- 115g sugar
- 100g macadamia nuts
- 1 egg
- 1 egg yolk
- ½ tsp vanilla essence or 2 tsps rum
- 2 tbsps caster sugar, extra

Pastry

- 190g plain flour
- Pinch of salt
- 100g unsalted butter
- 1 egg yolk
- 2-3 tbsps iced water

You can use frozen shortcrust pastry

Method

Pre-heat oven to 180°C. Place the almonds and macadamia nuts on a lined baking tray and roast in the oven for a couple of minutes until golden; set aside to cool. To make the pastry, sift flour and salt into a bowl, rub butter into flour until the mixture resembles breadcrumbs, stir in egg yolk and enough water to bind pastry. Turn dough onto lightly floured surface, knead gently, wrap in plastic wrap and refrigerate for 20 minutes.

Roll out pastry onto a lightly floured surface to 3 millimetres thick and transfer to a lightly greased pie dish, trim edges, prick bottom and refrigerate while you make the filling. To make the filling, place almonds in a food processor and pulse until fine, add the flour. In a separate bowl, cream the butter and sugar using an electric mixer until light and creamy. Gradually beat in egg yolk and egg, stir in almond mix, crushed macadamia nuts and vanilla. Spoon filling evenly into pastry case. Cut apples into slices and arrange on tart in a pattern. Press into tart gently.

Place tart into oven for 10-15 minutes until pastry begins to brown. Lower heat to 160°C and continue baking for a further 15 minutes or until nut cream filling is set. 10 minutes before the end of the cooking time, sprinkle the tart with remaining sugar and return to the oven. Serve hot with cream.

Wattleseed

Acacia species - Mimosaceae Family

Wattleseed has to be the unsung hero of the Australian native food industry. Acacias with their enormous diversity of species and forms cover the length and breadth of the Australian continent, and although not all acacias are suitable for human consumption, they have been a mainstay in the diet of indigenous Australians for thousands of years. The wattle flower is the well-known emblem of Australia, and is represented in the green and gold worn by Australian athletes.

Several species of acacias are more palatable and commercially viable: Acacia victoriae (prickly acacia), Acacia sophorae (coastal wattle), Acacia retinodes (wirilda), Acacia coriacea (dogwood), Acacia murrayana (colony wattle) and Acacia aneura (mulga).

In their natural habitats these species are plentiful and accordingly have been mainly harvested in the wild. The most sought-after wattleseed is Acacia retinodes (wirilda), which is now being planted in large commercial plots for the bushfood industry. The seeds have very hard husks, and when they fall to the ground will last for up to 20 years in their natural environment, usually only germinating after bushfires.

Because the hard outer casing also protects the seed during long periods of dormancy on the ground, wattleseed has provided indigenous Australians with a rich source of protein and carbohydrate in times of drought. The seed was crushed into flour between flat grinding stones and cooked into cakes or damper. Even the green seeds of some species were eaten after baking in hot coals.

Roasted or ground wattleseed has a diverse number of uses in the kitchen from baking to thickening sauces, and from use in casseroles to ice-cream. By dark roasting wattleseed, the most delightful aroma of nutty fresh roasted coffee is released and can be used as a beverage or as an addition to chocolate or desserts.

To order wattleseed, simply go to *www.theoutbackcafe.com*

Baked Wattleseed Cheesecake

Ingredients

- 1 packet sweet biscuits
- 150g melted butter
- 250g ricotta cheese
- 150g cottage cheese
- 2 tsps lemon or lime rind
- 1 tbsp semolina
- 2 tbsps buttermilk
- 3 eggs (separated)
- ¾ cup caster sugar
- 2 tbsps wattleseed

Method

Pre-heat oven to 180˚C.

Crush biscuits in a large bowl. Slowly incorporate the butter and mix to combine.

Press into the base of a lightly greased 24 centimetre spring form tin, chill until firm.

To make the filling, beat the cheeses, rind, semolina, buttermilk, egg yolks and wattleseed with an electric mixer.

In a separate bowl, beat the egg whites, slowly adding the sugar until it forms soft peaks.

Fold the egg whites into the cheese mixture to combine. Pour mixture over biscuit base and bake in oven for 1 hour.

Tower Hill

VICTORIA

Tourism Victoria

You'll love every piece of Victoria

KBN
Koori business network

Tourism Australia

Directions from Melbourne: take the Princes Highway to Geelong, then some 5km south of Geelong join the Great Ocean Road to Torquay, Anglesea, Lorne, Apollo Bay, Point Campbell, Peterborough and Warrnambool. Tower Hill is located 15km west of Warrnambool.

Tower Hill

Nestled in the crater of a dormant volcano, Tower Hill Reserve in south-west Victoria is a haven for wildlife, a fascinating ecological site and a showcase for local indigenous culture. Within its broad crater rim a number of volcanic cones rise from a lake in a formation known as a nested maar. Artefacts found in the layers of exposed ash show that Aboriginal people were living in the area at the time of the eruption, some 30,000 years ago.

Although Tower Hill was declared Victoria's first National Park in 1892, the bush was eventually lost to farming and quarrying. A revegetation project began in the 1950s. Over several decades school children and other volunteer groups planted thousands of trees. As the bush returned, so did the wildlife.

Today, Worn Gundidj Co-operative, in co-operation with Parks Victoria, has revitalised Tower Hill. It is now a thriving nature reserve and natural history centre where visitors can experience the bush, enjoy magnificent scenery, see Australian birds and animals (such as emus, koalas, kangaroos, wallabies, echidnas, black swans, wedge-tail eagles and magpie geese) in their natural habitat and learn about local indigenous culture.

Among the many nature walks are the 30 minute Peak Climb to the highest peak in the park, where there is a breathtaking view over the whole expanse of Tower Hill, the 45 minute Hat Island Habitat Track through blackwoods, gums, wattles and sheoaks and a growing diversity of plant life reintroduced under the revegetation program, and a one-hour Journey to the Last Volcano walk where visitors learn about the origins of Tower Hill and what makes it one of the most remarkable geological features of the western Victorian volcanic plain.

Tower Hill Reserve and visitors' centre is open every day (Monday – Friday 9am – 5pm, weekends and public holidays 10am – 4pm) and entry is free.

Worn Gundidj Aboriginal Co-operative

Established in 1992 to provide employment opportunities for indigenous people and their families within community-based enterprises, the co-operative's activities include job matching, product creation, nature-based tourism, cultural interpretation and saleable items, and a wholesale nursery, land rehabilitation programs and bush food.

**1-3 Rooneys Road, Warrnambool, VIC 3280.
Phone (03) 5561 5315 email: admin@worngundidj.org.au
website: www.worngundidj.wias.net.au**

Other attractions in Tower Hill

While in the area, visit Cheeseworld, 5330 Great Ocean Road, Allansford, the home of award-winning cheddar cheeses, where there is complimentary cheese tasting daily, a museum featuring relics from early 1900s farm life, and a licensed restaurant that specialises in country-style meals. At the Trout Farm, 221 Wollaston Road, visitors are guaranteed to catch locally grown fish. All equipment is supplied, and no licence is needed.

Mark took the opportunity while visiting Tower Hill to prepare one of his favourite dishes — his outback pizza, featuring kangaroo prosciutto, goats cheese and lemon myrtle. In this rich volcanic area, indigenous people had access to a wide variety of foods — wallaby and kangaroo, emu, echidna and koala, as well as seafood, sea parsley, lemon myrtle and many other native herbs, spices and fruits.

Yabbie Salad with Black Olive Dressing

Ingredients

- 6 yabbie tails
- 1 packet fresh gourmet salad mix
- Handful fresh rocket leaves
- 2 roma tomatoes
- 1 Lebanese cucumber

Salad dressing

- 80ml olive oil
- 40ml balsamic vinegar
- 30ml lemon/lime juice
- 1 tsp wattleseed (roasted)
- 1 tsp kutjera powder
  (crushed desert raisins)

Method

Blanch yabbie tails in boiling water until pink. Remove heads and peel shell off tails, leave ends. Set aside in fridge. Finely chop lettuce, rocket, tomatoes and cucumber.

To make the dressing, place all ingredients in a small bowl and stir to combine. Dress salad and leave for 5-8 minutes, adding tails to absorb flavour.

Arrange salad on plate and serve.

Serves 2.

Bush Tucker Pizza with Kangaroo Apple Relish

Ingredients

- 1 cup dried desert raisins, soaked overnight and roughly chopped
- ½ cup kangaroo apples or cumquats, roughly chopped
- 2 x 400g tin crushed tomatoes
- 1 medium sized onion, finely diced
- 3 medium sized tomatoes, diced
- 2 dstspns tomato paste
- 1 cup of water
- ½ cup white vinegar
- 2 tbsps olive oil
- ½ cup sugar
- 5 cloves, ground
- 1 cinnamon stick
- 1 dstspn dried saltbush
- Salt and pepper to taste

Pizza Base

- 1 tsp dry yeast
- 1 dstspn olive oil
- ½ cup warm water
- 1 ½ cups plain flour
- Salt and pepper to taste

Topping

- 1 kangaroo fillet
- ½ thinly sliced red capsicum
- Rocket lettuce (small handful)
- ½ thinly sliced Spanish onion
- 50g goats cheese
- Saltbush

Method

Relish: Grind the cloves and the pepper using a mortar and pestle. Heat oil in a frypan and cook onions until golden. Add the tinned tomatoes, tomato paste, desert raisins, kangaroo apples, pepper and cloves, vinegar, water, sugar, cinnamon stick, saltbush and chopped tomatoes and simmer for 30-40 minutes, stirring regularly (add a little extra water if necessary). Set aside in fridge.

Pizza Base: Combine yeast and warm water in a small bowl, stir until dissolved. Combine flour, salt and pepper and olive oil in a large bowl and slowly add the yeast mixture to form a soft dough (you may need to add more flour if the mixture is too moist). Set aside in a warm place and let the dough rise. After 20 minutes knock it back and set aside for a further 20 minutes before rolling out the dough.

Topping: Sear the kangaroo fillet in a hot saucepan in a small amount of olive oil, browning the outside. Finely slice and set aside. Turn dough onto floured surface; knead until smooth and roll out onto a pizza tray. Spread the relish onto the dough and then arrange the topping ingredients, finally crumbling on the goats cheese and a sprinkle of salt bush. Place in oven pre-heated to 220°C for about 10-15 minutes.

Wattleseed Swirl Ice-Cream

Ingredients

- 2 cups milk
- 1 cup of thickened cream
- ¼ cup sugar
- 3 egg yolks
- 2 dstspns of
  roasted ground wattleseed

Method

Steep wattleseed in boiling water (to swell) and set aside to cool. Beat the egg yolks in a large bowl. Add sugar intermittently and beat until thick and creamy. Heat the milk and cream in a saucepan. Fold the egg and sugar mixture into the milk and cream, a little at a time to prevent curdling. Stir and cook until thick and creamy. Set aside to cool, and then place in the fridge for an hour.

Pour mixture and wattleseed into an ice-cream churner and churn for approximately one hour until it doubles in size. Place ice-cream mixture into a container and freeze for about 10 hours or until set.

Makes 500ml.

Margaret River

WESTERN AUSTRALIA

BUNBURY

Busselton

Margaret River

Augusta • Pemberton •

Manjimup

Tourism
WESTERN AUSTRALIA

Tourism Australia

Margaret River
SOUTH-WEST WESTERN AUSTRALIA

Western Australia's Margaret River region is today renowned as one of Australia's premier wine-producing regions. Its transformation from a dairying and agricultural region since European settlement has been quite dramatic, bringing tourists and significant new investment and development to the area in the past 30 years.

The connection Aboriginal people have had with the region goes back many thousands of years.

The Tall Tuart Forest of Ludlow is part of the tribal lands of the Wardandi people, and is an area of special significance to their culture. As a relatively open forest with a scattered understorey, the area was easy to move through and was an ideal location for large camps and tribal gatherings.

The French witnessed this in 1801 when they visited the area and noted the Ludlow forest as a massive tribal council ground where the governing of the people took place. Local Aboriginal elder Bill Webb has described the typical scene as numerous camps spread throughout the forest, with the campfire light reflecting off the white bark of the tuarts in a way that lit up the area and allowed people to walk from camp to camp with ease.

Before European settlement, the tuart forest was dominated by many more large tuarts, and it is therefore not surprising that the area was used by the Wardandi people as a gathering point for tribal meetings with other people of the Bibbulmun Nation such as the Koreng, Wilman, Minang, Ballardong and Pibelmen. When such meetings took place, the different tribes camped around a common elders' circle with each tribe located around this circle like points of a compass, pointing towards the direction of their tribal lands.

William Hayward, a young member of the Wardandi people, tells visitors how the Ludlow Tall Tuart Forest is still close to the heart of the Wardandi people. They have a strong connection to the sea, and are custodians of many caves in the area. The caves are passages to the afterlife and the region of the sea god, Wardan.

The Wardandi people have developed the Wardan Aboriginal Cultural Centre as a place where they introduce their culture to visitors, school groups and Aboriginal people from other areas. Activities have been designed to bring about a greater understanding of the historical, social and environmental issues affecting Australians. A one-kilometre walk trail has been enhanced with bush tucker and medicine plants and traditional structures (mia-mia). There are also toolmaking and spear throwing workshops, as well as art, music and dance demonstrations.

The Wardan Aboriginal Centre is located three hours south of Perth on Injidup Springs Road off Wyadup Road, six kilometres south of Yallingup and one and a half kilometres west of Caves Road. The Centre is about 30 minutes travel time from Busselton and 30 minutes from Margaret River.

The instructors are elders and cultural custodians of the Wardandi cultural group, the traditional custodians of the lands from Busselton to Augusta. The program is located at the Wardan Aboriginal Cultural Centre, a 40-acre bush property 6km South of Yallingup.

There are three principle areas of teaching (geared to appropriate levels).

Mark Olive's visit to Margaret River enabled him to see sea celery (also called sea parsley) growing freely along the coastline. Mark uses the ingredient, which is high in Vitamin C, as a garnish and/or flavouring for pasta and drinks. The Wardandi people retain their strong links to the sea, and this focus provided Mark with numerous opportunities to produce some tantalising dishes using traditional herbs and spices.

Lemon Myrtle Barramundi

Ingredients

- 1 cup white rice
- ½ tsp turmeric powder
- 10 strands saffron
- 250g barramundi fillet
- 50g butter
- ½ cup plain flour
- 6 green grapes

Sauce

- 10g butter
- ½ cup thickened cream
- Lemon myrtle
- ½ cup white wine
- Lemon wedge

Method

Place 3 cups of water in a saucepan to boil and add the rice, turmeric and saffron. Simmer until the rice has absorbed all the water. Press rice into mould (optional) and set aside.

Coat the barramundi fillet with a dusting of flour. Melt butter in a shallow saucepan until it begins to bubble, add the fillet presentation side first. Cook until golden brown, then turn and cook for a further minute. Transfer to an oven tray and place in oven pre-heated to 180°C for 5-10 minutes while you prepare the white wine sauce.

To make the sauce, heat butter in a saucepan, add the thickened cream and simmer until it starts to reduce. Add the white wine and reduce by half. Just before serving, add a pinch of salt and pepper, lemon myrtle and the juice of the lemon wedge. To serve, turn out rice onto a heated plate. Place the barramundi fillet on the plate, cover with sauce and garnish with grapes.

Butter Fried Abalone Salad

Ingredients

- 1 green lipped abalone or
  2 roe-eyed abalone
- ½ cup sweet soy sauce
- Juice of 1 small lemon and lime
- 30ml fish sauce
- 25g butter
- Rocket lettuce
- 2 truss tomatoes (thinly sliced)

Dressing

- 100ml olive oil
- 80ml white wine vinegar
- 2 teaspoons wattleseed
- Juice of ½ a lemon
- Salt and pepper to taste

Method

Remove the abalone from the shell and clean well. Once cleaned softly hit the abalone with a mallet to break down and soften the muscle, then slice into very thin slices (like scalloped chips). Set aside.

In a bowl add the soy sauce, lemon and lime juice, salt and pepper and fish sauce. Pour over the abalone and set aside to marinate for at least 2 hours.

Meanwhile, to prepare the dressing, place all the ingredients in a small bowl and mix well. In a hot shallow saucepan melt the butter and fry off the abalone for about 30 seconds.

Pile cooked abalone, on a bed of rocket and sliced tomatoes and drizzle on the wattleseed dressing.

Serves 2.

Flash Damper

Ingredients

- 2 cups of plain flour
- 2 cups self-raising flour
- 50g butter
- 1 cup milk
- 1 cup water
- 1 dstspn sea parsley
- 1 dstspn dried saltbush
- Salt and pepper to taste

Method

Pre-heat oven to 180°C. Combine flours, sea parsley and saltbush in a large bowl. Melt butter in a saucepan, add the water and milk (do not boil). Slowly incorporate the liquid mixture into the flour mixture until just combined. Turn out onto a lightly floured surface and knead lightly (do not over knead as it will toughen). With some flour, roll the dampers into a dinner roll size, place them on a greased tray, brush top of dough with milk and sprinkle with some sea parsley. Place in oven for 15-20 minutes or until golden brown.

Makes 6-8 dampers.

Kakadu

NORTHERN TERRITORY

NORTHERN TERRITORY
travelnt.com

Tourism Australia

Kakadu community

Kakadu National Park lies 133 kilometres, or some two hours' drive east of Darwin, and is known for its postcard-perfect escarpment that carves through lush wetlands, savannah woodland and monsoon forest. At its centre is the small mining township of Jabiru, the only Australian town set inside a national park. Covering an area of more than 19,000 square kilometres, Kakadu is the largest national park in Australia and one of the largest in the world. The diversity of nature contained within the park is astounding, including waterfalls, gorges, water-lilied billabongs, paperbark forests and vast grasslands.

But Kakadu isn't just an icon for its environment. The park has a rare dual World Heritage listing for both its natural assets and its Aboriginal culture, which dates back some 50,000 years. The original Aboriginal inhabitants of Kakadu, the Gagadju people, left behind a treasure trove of rock art and paintings. Some of the earliest examples are thought to be at least 20,000 years old, or even dating back 35,000 years. More than 5000 have been recorded, and the most famous examples of these are at Nourlangie Rock and Ubirr.

Kakadu protects a rich variety of flora and fauna, including many rare and endangered species. Sixty four mammal and marsupial species, including wallabies, quolls, dingoes and wild horses, have been recorded and Kakadu also supports more than 280 bird species — about one-third of all bird species found in Australia, making it a magnet for bird watchers. Some bird species range over a number of habitats, but many are found in only one environment. Peaceful doves and red-collared lorikeets are widespread, while black-banded pigeons, white-lined honeyeaters and yellow chats occupy localised habitats. In the dry season, it's estimated that more than 60 percent of the world's magpie geese descend on the park and in total about three million birds might be seen at a time.

To date, more than 117 species of reptiles have been recorded in Kakadu, including goanna and monitor species, lizards and skinks and 39 snake species. Two species of crocodile are found in Kakadu: the freshwater crocodile (Crocodylus johnstonii) and the infamous estuarine, or saltwater, crocodile (C. porosus). 'Freshies', as they're called locally, grow to three metres, whereas 'salties' can exceed six metres in length.

There are six main landforms in Kakadu National Park: the Stone Country, which includes the Arnhem Land plateau and escarpment complex; the Outliers; the Lowlands, known as the Koolpinyah Surface; the Southern Hills and Basins; the Floodplains; and the Tidal Flats.

During the wet season, water carried down from the Arnhem Land plateau often overflows from creeks and rivers onto nearby floodplains. The most accessible places to view the floodplains are at Yellow Water, Mamukala, Iligadjarr, Ubirr and Bubba wetland.

Mark Olive's visit to Kakadu centred on the main township of Jabiru, where, at the local community centre, he prepared dishes featuring barramundi, emu, kangaroo and a wonderful tandoori crocodile recipe that attracted huge interest. Mark also used sugar bag honey that is collected from small native bees (that don't sting) and which is particularly sweet and suitable as an accompaniment to many dishes.

Macadamia and Mustard Wallaby Stack

Ingredients

- 500g wallaby steaks (butterfly cut)
- 1 sweet potato, thinly sliced lengthways
- 1 zucchini, thinly sliced lengthways
- 1 capsicum, cut into 4 equal pieces
- Native mountain pepper
- 3 dstspns seeded mustard
- 1 dstspn honey
- ¼ cup crushed macadamia nuts

Method

Pre-heat oven to 200°C. Prepare steaks in a butterfly cut, coat with native mountain pepper. Coat the zucchini, sweet potato, and capsicum with olive oil and cook on a hot griddle plate until tender and sprinkle with native mountain pepper. Remove from griddle and set aside. Sear both sides of the wallaby steak quickly on a very hot griddle until medium rare then set aside. On a baking tray, layer the sweet potato, zucchini, capsicum and wallaby, repeat. Top with crushed macadamia nuts and place in oven until nuts are golden brown. **Sauce** Mix the seeded mustard and honey in a small bowl. Place the stack on a plate and drizzle with the honey mustard sauce. Sprinkle native mountain pepper around the plate and add some whole roasted macadamia nuts for presentation. Serves 4.

Tandoori Crocodile Sticks

Ingredients

- 1kg crocodile fillet
- 400g plain yoghurt
- 3 dstspns tandoori paste
- Juice of ½ a lemon and lime
- 1 tsp native pepperberry
- Salt to taste

Method

Mix the yoghurt, tandoori paste, lemon juice, lime juice, salt and pepperberry in a bowl.

To prepare the skewers, cut the crocodile into strips and thread onto soaked bamboo skewers. Place skewers in a baking tray and spread on the marinade. Leave overnight or for a couple of hours to marinate. Grill on a hot plate for 1 minute each side.

Serve on a bed of rocket and steamed rice with a lemon wedge.

Serves 4.

Sugarbag Honey Crumble

Ingredients

Crumble topping
- 1 cup plain flour
- 50g butter
- 1 cup coconut
- ¾ cup brown sugar

Stewed Apples and Plums
- 3 green apples and 3 plums
- ½ cup of water
- Juice of 1 lemon
- 1 cup muntrie berries
- 50ml honey (sugar bag if available)

Method

Pre-heat oven to 180°C. In a bowl, rub butter and flour together between your fingers until mixture forms a crumbly texture and holds together with a squeeze. Add the brown sugar and coconut, mix through and set aside.

Peel, core and roughly chop the apples and chop the plums. Place the apples in a saucepan, cover with water and cook until soft. Add the plums, lemon juice, muntrie berries and honey. Simmer on a slow heat for a further 2 minutes.

Transfer apple mix to small oven proof bowls and top with the crumble mixture. Bake in oven for 15-20 minutes or until golden brown.

Serves 4.

Magnetic Island

QUEENSLAND

Ingham

Magnetic Island

TOWNSVILLE

Ayr

Tourism Tropical
North Queensland

Great
Tropical
Drive

Townsville Enterprise

Promoting North Queensland
REGIONAL DEVELOPMENT · TOURISM · CONVENTIONS · EVENTS

Tourism Australia

Magnetic Island

OFF TOWNSVILLE, NORTH QUEENSLAND

Magnetic Island, just 25 minutes by fast catamaran from Townsville, is a wilderness playground as well as a fast-growing community and the ancestral home of the Wulgurukaba people. Once part of the North Queensland mainland, Magnetic Island became isolated from the coast when the sea level rose about 7500 years ago, flooding the low-lying woodland between Townsville and the island. Consequently, a unique and diverse suite of plants and animals have evolved, with some species thought to be endemic.

Three-quarters of Magnetic Island is national park and is a part of the Great Barrier Reef World Heritage Area. Consequently, these different ecosystems result in an abundance of flora and fauna including huge strands of eucalyptus trees, a colony of koalas, Allied rock-wallabies, brushtail possums and a plethora of birdlife including white-bellied sea-eagle, sulphur-crested cockatoos and bush stone-curlews.

There are 23 beautiful beaches and bays around the island, many of which are not usually frequented by tourists or even locals due to their relative inaccessibility to most but the adventurous. Visitors who venture off the beaten track with Aboriginal botanist Warren Whitfield on a Great Green Way

Eco Tour or Fire Stick Tour visit Horseshoe Bay, Alma Bay, Geoffrey Bay, Nelly Bay, Picnic Bay and Cockle Bay where they see wallabies, a wonderful array of birdlife and maybe even a koala. Warren provides a detailed and informative commentary and demonstrations about indigenous culture, bush foods, medicines and traditional firemaking.

Magnetic Island is the only Great Barrier Reef Island that offers a wide range of accommodation and holiday houses with up market 4-5 star resort-style properties coming on line. Tropical-style resorts, units and backpacker establishments are also currently available. This extensive choice of accommodation, natural attractions and activities give the island its characteristic charm and laid-back holiday atmosphere. Magnetic Island is home to monthly full moon parties and other activities including beach horseriding, parasailing, snorkelling, diving, water activities, golf, tennis, reef and fishing trips. Discover the heritage of the island on the Forts Walk, the heritage trails on Arcadia and Picnic Bay and the maritime history of the nine different shipwrecks (Magnetic Island has close to 30km of walking trails to explore).

The ferry and vehicle barge that connects Magnetic Island and Townsville operates 15 times daily, ensuring easy access to this wilderness wonderland.

Mark Olive's visit to Magnetic Island gave him a close-up look at island life, as well as the many varied and interesting foods available there. Mark cooked wallaby with roasted vegetables, cedared mustard and native honey. He also found that there is an abundance of seafood and many interesting plants such as finger limes which can be used in many different dishes.

Grilled Pepper Roo in a Sweet Rosella Jus

Ingredients

- 250g kangaroo fillet
  (or scotch fillet, eye fillet)
- 2 tsps native mountain pepper
- Olive oil
- 1 cup wild rice

Sauce

- ½ cup beef stock
- Salt and pepper
- 1½ tsps rosella jam
- ½ cup red wine
- 2 rosella flowers in syrup, finely
  chopped (one extra for presentation)

Method

Pre-heat oven to 180˚C. Coat kangaroo in native mountain pepper. Heat a griddle or heavy based frying pan until hot, brush with a little olive oil and sear the kangaroo fillet for a couple of minutes on each side. Transfer fillet to the oven for 10 minutes. Meanwhile, bring a large saucepan of salted water to the boil, add the wild rice and cook. Drain and set aside.

To make the sauce, heat the stock in a saucepan, season with salt and pepper, add rosella jam and simmer for a couple of minutes. Add red wine, rosella flowers (including syrup), stir and simmer for a further minute to reduce slightly.

To serve, cut kangaroo fillet thinly across the grain, arrange on a bed of wild rice, drizzle with the rosella jus and garnish with a rosella flower. Serves 2.

Lemon Myrtle Linguini with Creamed Mussels

Ingredients

- 12 mussels, cleaned with beards removed
- ½ packet linguini
- 1 tsp lemon myrtle
- 1 cup cream
- Juice of 1 lemon
- Salt and pepper
- ½ cup white wine
- 4 shallots, finely sliced

Method

Bring a large saucepan of salted water to the boil, add linguini and lemon myrtle and cook until al dente. Drain and set aside.

Meanwhile, heat cream and half the wine in a saucepan, season with salt and pepper, add mussels and simmer for 5 minutes. Remove mussels from pan and set aside. Add lemon juice and remaining wine to the pan; simmer for a couple of minutes until slightly thickened. Return mussels to pan and stir in shallots.

To serve, arrange mussels on the pasta and cover with sauce.

Serves 2.

Cheese-free Cheesecake with a Drizzling of Quandong and Noni Syrup

Ingredients

Base
- 1 packet Granita biscuits
  (or other oat/wheat biscuits)
- 40g butter, melted

Filling
- 1 packet gelatine
- 1 cup warm water
- 1 cup cream
- ½ cup sugar
- 375ml natural yoghurt

Syrup Topping
- ½ cup noni juice
- ¼ cup sugar
- 2 tsps chopped quandongs
- 5 dstspns passionfruit pulp

Method

Dissolve gelatine in water, set aside in fridge to cool. Crush biscuits in a large bowl until they resemble breadcrumbs. Slowly incorporate the butter to combine. Press over base of lightly greased spring form tin, chill until firm.

To make the filling, beat cream with electric mixer, slowly add sugar and beat until it forms soft peaks.

Add yoghurt to gelatine mixture and whisk well. Slowly fold the gelatine mixture into the cream and mix to combine. Pour mixture over biscuit base, cover and refrigerate overnight until set.

To make the topping, heat noni juice in a saucepan, add sugar and quandongs and simmer for a couple of minutes. Stir in passionfruit pulp and simmer for a further minute. Cut cheesecake into slices and serve with a drizzle of the quandong and noni syrup.

Tully & Daintree

TROPICAL NORTH QUEENSLAND

INNISFAIL

Tully •

Ingham •

Tourism Tropical
North Queensland

Great
Tropical
Drive

Promoting North Queensland
Townsville Enterprise
REGIONAL DEVELOPMENT • TOURISM • CONVENTIONS • EVENTS

Tourism Australia

Tully & Daintree

TROPICAL NORTH QUEENSLAND

Tropical Queensland is home to some of the most interesting and distinctive Aboriginal cultures in Australia.

For many thousands of years, Tropical Queensland has had the highest indigenous population density in Australia. More than 20 different tribal groups and over 60 clan groups co-exist in this rich tropical landscape.

Their traditional lifestyle has evolved in tropical forests over many thousands of years, and sets them apart from other Aboriginal groups. The Rainforest Aboriginal people – the Bama – make giant wooden shields, cross-boomerangs and axes, weave beautiful baskets and build single outrigger canoes. They also use unusual methods of hunting and trapping in the lush rainforest, and have special ways of processing poisonous rainforest fruits.

Mark Olive discovered the continuing deep ties between Aboriginal people and the rainforest as he followed the Great Tropical Drive from Townsville to Cooktown. "I found the land continues to provide physical sustenance – but I also felt spiritually nourished by the wisdom of the elders and their connection to their country," he says.

There are more than 30 indigenous tourism experiences in Tropical Queensland, including cultural centres, dance theatres, festivals and rainforest tours. If you walk into a forest and see trees, you're not getting the full picture. Take a walk with a rainforest Aboriginal guide and you'll have a completely different experience.

The Echo Creek Walking Track in Tully Valley is a tour owned and operated by local rainforest Aboriginal people who built the track and now guide visitors on a half-day tour. Team leader Robert Grant has spent more than 20 years working on nearby banana farms, and is enjoying working for himself in the bush he loves. "We spent our childhood running around and living in the bush," he says, "so we all really loved getting in here and clearing up the track. We've kept it looking very natural, so that people can get close to nature."

The trail follows a traditional Aboriginal trading route from the coast over the coastal range to the tablelands. Robert and several other guides take groups for a half-day walk through the forest, identifying the many different rainforest species by both their Aboriginal and botanical names, and describing their traditional uses as bush tucker and medicines. The trail passes carpets of lush moss beside peaceful healing pools where fish and turtles swim.

Visitors finish up having lunch and a swim at the base of a waterfall deep in the rainforest. Not all are prepared for the stillness and strength that pervades these ancient tropical forests. "We help people to look at the bush through our eyes," Robert explains. "We tell them how Aboriginal people used to live and walk around in the rainforest. We also explain how there are many Aboriginal language groups in the rainforest, and each one is different. We all have our own language and culture."

The Echo Creek Walking Track is linked to the King Ranch Cultural Centre which has a cultural amphitheatre, art gallery and fascinating collection of artifacts from local Aboriginal people and early settlers.

Echo Creek Walking Track & King Ranch Cultural Centre, phone (07) 4068 0424.

Other attractions

The Jirrbal people's fascinating traditional lifestyle is showcased in the Nganyaji Cultural Centre at the Ravenshoe Visitor Centre. The centre's displays begin with "country" and then moves to "Jujuba creation time" which tells the stories of the establishment of Jirrbal lore and society.

Displays about traditional lifestyles include rainforest base-camp villages, rainforest cuisine and community life. Other displays feature the story of contact with Europeans and finally, the Jirrbal people today. Nganyaji Cultural Centre is designed to create an awareness that traditional life is not something in the distant past. Significant elements of this lifestyle continue within the living memory of Ravenshoe's residents. The centre is open 9am to 4pm, seven days a week.

Daintree region

The Daintree region to the north of Cairns is the traditional homeland of the Kuku Yalanji people. Yalanji children still learn their traditional language and Yalanji cultural traditions and ties to the land are very strong.

There are several excellent indigenous experiences for visitors. Take a walk in lush rainforest to learn about Yalanji culture, bush tucker and medicine. Along the way, green ants provide an interesting story of how they are used medicinally for the symptoms of colds – they have a citrus, lemony flavour, high in vitamin C.

At the waterfall are king ferns with fronds eight metres long which date back 400 million years. Cycad palms that grow only one centimetre a year also share this unique environment with the 600 million year-old zamia ferns which have an unusual underground trunk system, believed to have evolved as an adaptation against browsing dinosaurs. Aboriginal art and cultural workshops include an insight into traditional artefact-making and Aboriginal storytelling through paintings.

Guests at Daintree Eco Lodge and Spa experience unique indigenous culture and traditions in every aspect of their stay. Bilngkumu Restaurant features natural ginger, coconut and bush foods in its recipes, and ingredients such as ochres, muds and ginger are among the treatments at the Daintree Spa.

Mark Olive's visit to Tully and Daintree enabled him to understand how indigenous rainforest people successfully lived off the land while living in a very different environment to other indigenous people on the Australian mainland. At Tully, Mark prepared a chilli potato gnocchi with broad beans and broccoli and native pepper, and in the Daintree he used local ingredients to put together a tantalising tropical salad with riberries and blue quandong.

Tropical Rainforest Salad

Ingredients

- 1 cup slithered almonds
- 1 tbsp desert flakes
- 1 small bunch rocket, finely chopped
- ¼ rockmelon, thinly sliced
- ¼ honeydew melon, thinly sliced
- ¼ pineapple, thinly sliced
- ½ red capsicum, finely sliced
- 1 cup muntrie berries
- ½ cup quondongs, chopped
- 1 packet salad mix

Dressing

- 2 tbsps olive oil
- 2 tbsps white wine vinegar
- ¼ cup orange juice
- ¼ cup pineapple juice
- Juice of ½ lemon
- Juice of ½ lime
- Salt and pepper, to taste

Method

Pre-heat oven to 200˚C.

Mix almonds and desert flakes on a roasting tray and roast in oven for 5 minutes.

In a large bowl, mix almonds, rocket, muntrie berries and quondongs.

Layer on a plate with salad mix, sliced melon, pineapple and capsicum.

To make the dressing, put ingredients in a small bowl, mix well and drizzle over the layered salad.

Pumpkin Gnocchi in a Mixed Bean and Tomato Sauce

Ingredients

- 1 cooked mashed butternut pumpkin
- 1 egg
- 2 cups plain flour
- 1 cup self-raising flour
- 1 tbsp mountain pepper
- Salt and pepper, to taste

Tomato Sauce

- ½ cup dried broadbeans
- 1 cup dried red kidney beans
- 50g butter
- 2 cloves garlic, crushed
- 1 onion, diced
- 2 tbsps plain flour
- 500g crushed tomatoes
- 2 tbsps native basil
- 1 tbsp saltbush
- 1 tsp pepperberry, crushed
- 1 tbsp chilli powder
- 3 tbsps tomato paste
- ⅓ cup vegetable stock

Method

Combine mashed pumpkin, mountain pepper, egg, salt and pepper in a large bowl. Mix well before gradually incorporating the flour, mixing until you have a soft dough. Tip onto a lightly floured bench and roll dough into a 2 centimetre thick roll. Cut into 2 centimetre even lengths and roll in a little extra flour. Rest for 30 minutes. Bring a large pot of salted water to the boil. Add gnocchi and cook until they rise to the surface – indicating they are cooked. Remove with a slotted spoon, drain well before adding to the sauce.

Tomato Sauce: Soak broadbeans and kidney beans overnight. Bring a large saucepan of water to the boil and cook beans until soft (approximately 20 minutes), drain and set aside.

Melt butter in saucepan and sauté the onion and garlic until soft. Add flour and mix thoroughly. Add herbs, crushed tomatoes, beans, tomato paste and stock and mix well. Bring to the boil and simmer for 10 minutes.

Serves 4 – 6.

Lemon and Ginger Barramundi with Sweet Potato Fries

Ingredients

- 2 barramundi fillets
- 2 lemons, thinly sliced
- 2 tbsps lemon myrtle
- 10 slices pickled ginger
- 2 sheets of paperbark
- 1 sweet potato
- Saltbush to taste
- Macadamia or olive oil, for frying

Method

Pre-heat oven to 180°C.

Lay fish fillets on paperbark. Score fillets and insert slices of pickled ginger. Layer with lemon slices and sprinkle with lemon myrtle. Fold the paperback over and tie with cooking/kitchen string, sprinkle with a little water to moisten. Bake in oven for 30 minutes.

To make the sweet potato fries, cut the sweet potato into chip portions, dry well with tea or paper towel. Fry chips in batches until brown and cooked through. Season with saltbush.

Serves 2.

Hopevale

TROPICAL NORTH QUEENSLAND

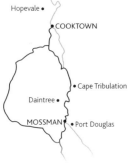
Hopevale •
• COOKTOWN

• Cape Tribulation
Daintree •
MOSSMAN • Port Douglas

Tourism Tropical
North Queensland

Great
Tropical
Drive

Townsville Enterprise
Promoting North Queensland
REGIONAL DEVELOPMENT • TOURISM • CONVENTIONS • EVENTS

Tourism Australia

Hopevale

Located 46 kilometres north of Cooktown in Far North Queensland, Hopevale is home to various clan groups who speak Guugu Yimithirr and other languages. Established as a Lutheran Mission in 1949, Aboriginal people from the Hope Valley and Cape Bedford Missions were settled there.

In 1986, the community became the first to receive a Deed of Grant in Trust (DOGIT) and formed the Hope Vale Aboriginal Council. In 1997, a Native Title determination was made concerning the lands of the Hope Vale DOGIT.

From the mid 1990s, the Great Barrier Reef Marine Park Authority (GBRMPA) and the Hopevale community worked together for three years to develop a community-based turtle and dugong hunting management plan for the region between Cape Melville and the Endeavour River at Cooktown. The plan, which was officially released in 1999, limits the number of dugong and turtles that can be taken and establishes rules to ensure that distress to the animals is minimised during and after capture. The plan, the first of its kind in Australia, was the culmination of 18 years' work by elders, traditional owners and other community members working in partnership with government agencies and researchers.

In 2000, the Hopevale community won the Prime Minister's Community Leadership Environmental Achievement Award for its work in developing the plan and the commitment to ensuring its success.

Les Gibson, of the Guugu Yimithirr people, has an unusual insight into the historic encounter with Captain James Cook and his crew who spent 48 days on the banks of the Wahalumbaal River repairing the Endeavour. The Guugu Yimithirr people supplied the crew with fresh meat, fish and another staples.

Les notes that the ramshackle encampment, now Cooktown, became the first European settlement on the Australian continent. During this time his ancestors' language became the first to be written down. The word kangaroo, for example, is derived from a Guugu Yimithirr word, Gangurru.

The Aboriginals had little use for trinkets offered by Cook in exchange for supplies. Nevertheless, they took them out of respect and curiosity. Les knows where some of these items are stored, placed in reverence in a secret cave along with huge painted murals documenting Cook's visit in the district. It is a secret Les is determined to keep.

Today, Guugu Yimithirr people refer to themselves as Bama and live at Hopevale.

Mark Olive's visit to Hopevale enabled him to learn how this community of some 3000 people live in a semi-remote area, and how – over many centuries – they developed a strong affinity with the land. The Guugu Yimithirr people were fortunate to have access to a wide variety of flora and fauna – wallabies, kangaroos, seafood, crocodile, as well as bird life and native fruits. Mark prepared dishes at Hopevale featuring mud crab, lemon myrtle and pandanus leaves.

Other attractions

While in the area, visitors have the opportunity to visit the Nugal-warra site in the company of Nugal-warra elder Wilfred (Willie) Gordon to hear the myths, legends and family history depicted in the art. Previously inaccessible to visitors, the sites are situated high in the hills above the Hope Vale community. Willie explains why the sites are of such importance to future generations of Nugal-warra people, gives his guests an understanding of the rich and complex society depicted in the art, and shares his ancient Aboriginal philosophy which shows how people can engage the environment in order to better understand themselves.

Tours include the Great Emu Tour (3.5 hours ex Cooktown, two hours ex Hopevale) which visits three rock art sites, including the Great Emu Cave, and the Rainbow Serpent Tour (5.5 hours ex Cooktown, 4 hours ex Hopevale) which takes visitors through a dramatic landscape to six rock art sites, including an ancestral birth cave and the Reconciliation Cave.

Smoked Emu Antipasto

Ingredients

Lebanese Bread Chips
- 1 packet Lebanese bread
- ¼ cup olive oil
- Desert flakes

Pickled Veggies
- 4 carrots, cut into thick sticks
- ½ cauliflower, cut into florets
- 1 red capsicum, cut into large diamonds
- 1 green capsicum, cut into large diamonds
- 1 red onion, cut into thick slices
- ¼ cup sugar
- ¼ cup white wine vinegar
- 1 glass Chardonnay
- 1 tbsp saltbush
- 1 tbsp mountain pepper

Method

Serve the Pickled Veggies and Lebanese Bread Chips recipes below as part of an antipasto platter with smoked emu, olives, cheese and dips.

Pre-heat oven to 180°C. Drizzle olive oil evenly over Lebanese bread, spread with a pastry brush. Sprinkle with desert flakes. Cut bread into even pieces (approximately 16 triangles) and bake in oven for 10-15 minutes or until crisp and golden.

Blanch carrot sticks and cauliflower florets in boiling salted water until al dente. Set aside to cool. Mix all vegetables together in a large glass bowl. Add sugar, vinegar and white wine. Sprinkle with mountain pepper and saltbush. Toss well, cover and refrigerate overnight (or at least 4 hours).

Chilli-Butter Crab and Emus on Humpbacks

Ingredients

Chilli-Butter Crab

- 4 blue swimmer crabs
- 1 tbsp olive oil
- 150g butter
- Juice of ½ lemon
- Juice of ½ lime
- Salt and pepper, to taste
- 1 tbsp chilli powder
- 1 cup white wine
- 1½ cups pineapple juice
- 100g chopped parsley
- 100g sliced shallots

Emus on Humpbacks

- 1 dozen oysters in ½ shells
- 100g sliced smoked emu
- 100ml Worcestershire Sauce
- 50g rocket

Method

Clean the crabs thoroughly and crack the shells. Heat butter and olive oil in a pan. Add crab, chilli powder, salt and pepper and sauté for 1 minute. Add white wine, pineapple juice, lemon and lime juice, mix well and cook for 5-10 minutes until crab turns red. Remove crab from pan and set aside, keep warm.

Strain liquid and return to pan, add parsley and shallots and reduce.

Pour sauce over crab and serve.

Emus on Humpbacks

Pre-heat oven to 180°C. Remove oysters from shells and rinse. Wrap each oyster in a slice of smoked emu using a toothpick to secure in place. Place back in shells and top with the Worcestershire Sauce. Place in oven for 5-10 minutes.

Top with a little chopped rocket and serve immediately while hot.

Serves 2.

Lemon Myrtle and Eucalyptus Shortbread

Ingredients

- 300g butter
- 2/3 cup caster sugar
- 3 ¼ cups plain flour
- 2/3 cup rice flour
- 1 tsp baking powder
- 1 tsp ground lemon myrtle

Icing

- 400g icing sugar
- 2 egg whites
- ½ tsp eucalyptus oil
- 2 tsps lemon juice

Method

Pre-heat oven to 160°C.

Sift flours, baking powder and lemon myrtle together in bowl.

Cream butter and caster sugar in a large bowl. Stir in flour mixture to form a soft dough. Cover with cling wrap and rest in the refrigerator for 30 minutes.

Roll dough out on a lightly floured surface to around 3 millimetres thickness. Cut into long fingers or triangles. Place on a greased oven tray and bake for 30 minutes or until shortbread is pale golden. Remove from tray and cool on wire rack.

To make the icing, beat egg whites until light and fluffy, fold in remaining ingredients and mix well. Ice cool biscuits and serve.

Makes approximately 20 biscuits.

Mark's Menus

Barbecue

Emu Kebabs

Ingredients

- 1kg emu fillet, cut into 2 cm cubes
  or chicken or lamb
- 2 onions, cut into wedges
- 1 red capsicum, cut into pieces
- 1 green capsicum, cut into pieces
- 12 small mushrooms

Marinade

- 1 tsp garlic, peeled and sliced
- ½ cup olive oil
- Juice from ½ a lemon
- Salt and pepper
- 1 small onion, finely diced
- 1 tsp pepperberry

Method

To make the marinade, combine all ingredients in a bowl and mix well.
Thread kangaroo, onion, capsicum and mushrooms alternately onto pre-soaked
skewers. Place on a baking tray, pour over marinade and set aside in refrigerator
for 1-2 hours. Barbeque skewers until cooked, brushing with the marinade and
turning frequently during cooking.
Serve immediately.

Marinated Lamb Chops

Ingredients

- 8 lamb chops
- 1 tsp native basil
- 1 tsp rivermint
- 1 clove garlic, crushed
- 3 tbsps rosella or apricot jam
- 2 tbsps soy sauce
- 1 tsp crushed ginger

Method

Cut excess fat off chops and set aside. Place the native basil, rivermint, garlic, jam, soy sauce and ginger into a blender and pulse until smooth. Pour mixture over the chops, cover and refrigerate overnight to marinade. Barbeque chops until cooked, brushing with the marinade during cooking.

BBQ Pork

Ingredients

- 500g pork fillets
- 1 tsp olive oil
- 1 clove garlic, crushed
- 2 tbsps dry sherry
- 1 tbsp honey
- 1 tbsp desert flakes
- 1 tbsp hoi sin sauce

Method

Mix olive oil, garlic, sherry, honey, desert flakes and hoi sin sauce together in a large bowl and mix well to combine. Place fillet into the marinade, cover and place in the refrigerator overnight to marinate. Barbeque the pork fillets, brushing with the marinade until cooked.
Serve with salad.

Brunch

Smoked Emu & Kutjera Omelette

Ingredients

- 100g shaved smoked emu or ham, roughly chopped
- Handful fresh spinach, roughly chopped
- 6 eggs, beaten
- ½ tsp kutjera powder
- 100g tasty cheese, grated
- Salt and pepper
- Olive oil for frying

Method

Heat a little olive oil in a fry pan, add the emu and spinach, stir. Add eggs and spices. While cooking push the edges of the omelette toward the centre, tilting the pan and pushing the uncooked eggs to the outer edge. Continue until the omelette is set but still creamy on the surface, sprinkle with cheese, cook for a few seconds, fold and slide onto a serving plate.

Serves 2.

Honeyed Yoghurt with Native Berries

Ingredients

- 500g tub natural or
  Greek style yoghurt
- 80-100ml native bee honey
  (regular honey is fine)
- 1 cup mixed native berries
  (or seasonal berries)

Method

Mix the honey and the yoghurt together in a bowl to combine. Stir through the berries and serve with cereal, crepes, fruit or on its own.
Serves 2.

Muntrie Berry Muffins with Lemon Myrtle Topping

Ingredients

- 180g plain flour
- 60g sugar
- 2 tsps baking powder
- ¼ tsp salt
- 2 eggs
- 55g butter, melted
- 175ml milk
- 1 tsp vanilla essence
- 1 tsp grated lemon rind
- 170g fresh muntrie berries or
  other seasonal berries

Topping

- ½ tsp lemon myrtle
- 1 cup icing sugar
- 1 egg yolk
- 2 tsps melted butter
- 1 tsp lemon juice

Method

Pre-heat oven to 180°C

Sift flour and baking powder into a large bowl, add sugar and salt. In a separate bowl whisk eggs, add melted butter, milk, vanilla and lemon rind. Add the wet ingredients to the dry ingredients and stir until just combined. Fold through the berries (do not over mix or muffins will be tough).

Spoon into a greased 12 cup muffin tin (or use paper cases) and bake in oven for 20-25 minutes or until tops spring back when touched lightly. Allow muffins to cool in pan for a few minutes before turning out onto a wire rack to cool.

To make the topping, combine all the ingredients in a bowl and mix well.

Once the muffins are cool, ice with the topping and serve.

Makes 12.

Long Lunch

Kangaroo Burgundy Pie

Ingredients

- 1kg kangaroo fillet, diced (or beef)
- 2 brown onions, diced
- 1 sweet potato, cut into 1cm cubes
- 1 cup red wine
- 3 cups beef stock
- Salt and pepper
- 2 tsps mountain pepper
- 1/3 cup flour
- 375g puff pastry sheets
- 2 tbsps olive oil for frying

Method

Pre-heat oven to 200°C. Heat the oil in a frypan and brown the kangaroo. Add onion, potatoes, 2 cups of stock, wine and mountain pepper. Cover and simmer for 1 hour or until meat is tender. Add salt and pepper to taste.

Mix flour with 1 cup of stock and add to meat mixture, stirring continuously until the sauce thickens. Set aside to cool.

Lay pastry sheet over pie dish and trim. Pour in cooled meat mixture, lay pastry sheet over top, seal the edge and trim away the excess. Glaze the top with egg wash and prick the top with a fork. Bake in oven for 10 minutes, then reduce the temperature to 180°C and bake for a further 20 minutes or until pastry is golden brown.

Serves 6.

Indigenous Style Spicy Paella

Ingredients

- 1/4 cup olive oil
- 1 large garlic clove, peeled and finely chopped
- 1 small Spanish onion, quartered
- 3 tomatoes
  (or 375ml crushed tomatoes)
- 1 red capsicum, finely sliced
- 1 fresh chilli
  (or 10 whole pepperberries)
- 2 rashers bacon, roughly chopped (optional)
- 2 bay leaves
- 1 1/3 cups long grain rice
- 1 tbsp lemon myrtle
- 1 tsp paprika
- Pinch of saffron
- 600ml fish stock

Ingredients *continued*

- 1 cup dry white wine
- 250g calamari rings
- 16 tiger prawns, peeled and de-veined (leave tails on)
- 250g Spanish mackerel (gemfish or any firm fish) cut into bite size pieces
- 12 black mussels
- Lemon or lime wedges for serving

Method

Heat oil in a deep frypan. Sauté garlic, onion, tomatoes, capsicum and chilli for 5 minutes until browned. Add bacon and bay leaves, cover and cook for a further 5 minutes. Add rice, lemon myrtle, paprika and saffron, mix well, add stock and wine, cover and simmer for 20 minutes stirring occasionally.

Place the seafood over the top of the rice mixture, adding more stock or water if needed. Cover and cook over a gentle heat until rice is tender and the seafood is cooked through.

Serve from pan at table with lemon wedges and crusty bread.

Serves 6.

Macadamia Nut Potato Salad with Capers

Ingredients

- 1kg chat potatoes
- ¼ cup macadamia nuts, roasted and chopped
- 4 shallots (finely sliced)
- 4 tsps small capers (drained)
- ½ tsp rivermint
- ½ tsp native basil
- 4 tbsps olive oil
- 2 tbsps red wine vinegar
- 1 tbsp lemon juice
- ½ red capsicum, diced
- ¼ tsp ground pepperberry

Method

Boil potatoes in a large saucepan until tender but firm (do not over cook). Quarter potatoes whilst warm and set aside in refrigerator to cool.

When potatoes are chilled, add capers, macadamia nuts, rivermint and native basil. In a small bowl, mix the oil, vinegar and lemon juice. Add onions and capsicum, season with salt and ground pepperberry. Pour over potatoes and toss gently to combine.

Aniseed Myrtle Biscotti with Coffee Shots

Ingredients

- 1¾ cup plain flour
- ²/₃ cup caster sugar
- ½ tsp baking powder
- 60g chilled unsalted butter, cubed
- 2 eggs
- 1¼ cups macadamia nuts, roasted and roughly chopped
- 2 tsps grated orange zest
- 1 tsp ground aniseed myrtle
- ½ tsp caster sugar, extra

Method

Pre-heat oven to 180°C.

Line two baking trays with baking paper.

In a food processor add sifted flour, sugar, baking powder and a pinch of salt. Mix for a couple of seconds then add butter and mix until the mixture resembles breadcrumbs. Add eggs and transfer to a floured surface. Knead in nuts, zest and aniseed myrtle and shape into two logs approximately 20 centimetre long. Place on a baking tray, sprinkle with sugar and bake for 20 minutes until golden brown.

Cut cooled logs into 1 centimetre diagonal slices, bake slices in oven for a further 15-20 minutes or until crisp.

Serve with coffee.

Drinks

Watermelon and Rivermint Granita

Ingredients

- 1 cup ice cubes
- 2 cups diced watermelon
- 1 tsp caster sugar
- ½ tsp rivermint

Method

Place all ingredients in a blender and blend until smooth.
Garnish with fresh fruit.

Lemon Myrtle & Ginger Tea

Ingredients

- 2 cups water
- 8 fresh/dried lemon myrtle leaves
- 5cm piece ginger, peeled and sliced
- 2 tsps honey

Method

Bring water to the boil, add lemon myrtle leaves, ginger and honey and simmer for 5 minutes.

Turn off heat, cover and allow to steep for a further 10 minutes (at least) to allow the flavours to infuse. Strain and serve.

Serves 2.

Variation

To make a refreshing summer thirst quencher, allow the tea to cool, and then add the juice of 2 oranges and some ice, stir and serve.

Wattleseed Mocha

Ingredients

- 60g good quality dark chocolate, chopped
- ½ cup cream
- 1 cup milk
- 1½ cups strong wattleseed espresso*
- 1 vanilla bean, split in half
- Ground nutmeg, for serving

Method

Place chocolate and cream in a saucepan. Stir over low heat until chocolate is melted. Stir in the milk, wattleseed espresso and vanilla bean. Continue to cook until hot. Do not boil. Pour into a glass and sprinkle with ground nutmeg. Add sugar to taste.

*To make the wattleseed espresso, mix 3 tablespoons of wattleseed with 1½ cups of boiling water in a plunger, allow to steep for 10 minutes.